# LEAVING THE LIGHT ON

*Building the memories that will draw your kids home*

# LEAVING THE LIGHT ON

## Gary Smalley
## & John Trent, Ph.D.

MULTNOMAH

LEAVING THE LIGHT ON

©1994 by Gary Smalley and John Trent

published by Multnomah Books

*a part of the Questar publishing family*

Contents based on material that appeared in a previous book,

entitled *Home Remedies: Timeless Prescriptions for Today's Family.*

*International Standard Book Number: 0-88070-620-1*
Cover design by David Uttley
Edited by Larry R. Libby


Printed in the United States of America.

For information:
QUESTAR PUBLISHERS, INC.
POST OFFICE BOX 1720
SISTERS, OREGON 97759


94 95 96 97 98 99 00 01—10 9 8 7 6 5 4 3 2 1

Smalley, Gary
Leaving the light on/Gary Smalley and John Trent.
p. cm.
ISBN 0-88070-620-1: $16.99
1. Family--Religious life. 2. Family-- United States. 3. United States--Moral Conditions
4. Christian life--1960—
I. Trent, John T. II. Title.
BV4526.2.S526 1994
248.4--dc20

94-502
CIP

# ACKNOWLEDGMENTS

To Larry Libby...our dear friend
and skilled editor who is so incredibly talented,
he can make even average rocks like us shine like diamonds.

And to Al Janssen for his special friendship
and for sharing his time and insights
at our initial book-planning retreat.

10⁴ᵉ

93/95

# CONTENTS

"Get Me Home" — 9

1. The Foundation for All Loving Relationships — 13

2. The Priceless Value of Affirmation — 25

3. Meaningful Touch — 37

4. Building Character and Responsibility — 49

5. "Are You Listening to Me?" — 61

6. Valuing Our Differences — 71

7. Blending Our Differences — 83

8. Untying the Knots of Anger — 95

9. Resolving Conflict — 105

10. The Glue That Bonds a Family — 115

11. How to Help Your Family Improve — 123

12. Preparing for Transitions — 135

13. Vision — 147

14. When a Child Walks Away from the Light — 157

15. When Life Overflows — 169

16. Watching for the Sunlight — 177

17. A Final Thought: Where Your Light Shines Best — 187

# INTRODUCTION

*Just let me get home, Lord.... Just let me get home.*

Daybreak over the Arabian desert looked calm and peaceful. Yet high above the desert floor, life was anything but calm for a pilot friend of ours during the Gulf War.

Captain Evans had already flown twenty combat sorties over Kuwait and Iraq in a war plane called the "Wart Hog." Twenty missions without a scratch...a record that was about to end.

Flying sortie number twenty-one against positions of the vaunted Iraqi Republican Guard, Evans's aircraft was suddenly ripped by 23mm cannon shells and small arms fire. The plane bucked under him and warning lights flashed inside his cockpit—something he hoped he would never see outside of a simulator.

The "Wart Hog," or A-10E, had earned its nickname by attacking ground targets at low altitudes, often in close support of infantry troops. Because it is designed to fly into the teeth of anti-aircraft and small arms fire, it is covered with armor. Pilots sit in a titanium protected "bathtub" to shield them from the pounding they could expect at that altitude.

Captain Evans's plane had indeed been pounded and now the war plane shuddered as it made its way back to base. He trailed a thin line of smoke, and feared his hydraulic system might fail at any moment. With rudders gone, the plane could slip into an irrecoverable spin.

Yet as part of the best-trained air force in the world, Evans forced aside the fear that crawled into the cockpit with him and made his mind go through a rigid checklist in preparation for an emergency landing.

Airspeed...check.

Altimeter...check.

Fuel levels…check.

    Family…check.

Hydraulic pressure…check.

ILS…check.

Flaps…check.

    Family…check.

In spite of himself, the one thought our friend couldn't hold captive was the one he treasured most of all…home. The picture of a loving wife and three children, the youngest only three, was zipped inside the top pocket of his flight suit.

*Just let me get home, Lord…. Just let me get home.*

The words echoed in his mind. Over and over.

Captain Evans's plane did touch down at his home base that morning sporting eighteen holes in his right wing and fuselage. Today he's back home with his family. But his story illustrates something we see in men and women across the country.

When the chips are down and we're battered by life, many of us find ourselves whispering, *Just let me go home, Lord…. Just let me go home. They'll love me…they'll care for me…they'll make everything all right….*

What kind of home do you want your children to look back on years from now? Are you turning on lights of love and laughter and shared dreams in your children's memories…lights that will tug at their thoughts and warm their hearts down the sometimes dark, sometimes winding roads of life?

In a loving home, there is hope and healing, help and health. Supportive arms hug away our hurts, voices cheer us on, smiles light up our eyes, and tears of compassion soothe us when we've failed. Even in the longest, darkest night, the porch light is always lit, always showing the way to the one place where love is given freely, not earned or demanded.

When it comes to the hurts we all face in life, the best place to turn is toward the lights of home. In fact, in the midst of our trials, God has designed a number of "home lighting" options that will bring warmth, brilliance, and beauty into our family rooms and dining rooms, bedrooms and play rooms. Bright lamps like unconditional affirmation, meaningful touch, hard earned wisdom, unquestioned character, and spiritual dependence. Together, they can move us past the darkness of our hurts and fears and safely on to the well-lighted regions of honesty, intimacy, and mutual respect.

Amidst the mad dash to reach the twenty-first century, we can still have close, loving families. It takes time and a commitment to caring. But with the right blend of knowledge, skills, and faith, you can provide the very things your children and spouse need so much.

In the pages that follow, you'll find more than a dozen time-tested concepts which can help you build a close-knit family. With God's help you can have the lightest, brightest home in the neighborhood. What did Jesus call it..."a light on a hill"?

So settle back now, grab a cup of coffee or tea and dip into some of the most important "light reading" you may ever experience. When those inevitable dark days come for you and your children, we think you'll be glad you did.

Gary Smalley, Branson, Missouri

Dr. John Trent, Phoenix, Arizona

# THE FOUNDATION FOR ALL LOVING RELATIONSHIPS

J uan watched for an opening, then ducked suddenly behind his teacher and darted out the door.

Kari shook her head as the dark-haired little boy raced down the hall and out of sight. This encounter at the door was becoming a daily challenge.

It was my (Gary's) daughter's first year of teaching second grade in a poor, inner-city district of Phoenix. Before Kari even began the year, she had determined that teaching was going to be more than an occupation.

For Kari, it was a mission. A calling. She felt specifically called by God to treasure the children in her class. As part of that process, she decided she would kneel at the door of her classroom at the end of every school day and give each child a smile, a hug, and a word of affection.

Juan tried his hardest to dodge Kari's attention. While she was hugging another child, he would try to squeeze through the door behind her. He couldn't meet her eyes, and he didn't want a hug.

At first Kari was puzzled. Didn't he like her? Was he embarrassed by

13

this display of tenderness? It was only after she did some looking into the little boy's background that she came up with the answer. Juan didn't want to be hugged because he felt he didn't *deserve* it. He felt so badly about himself that he couldn't accept someone else expressing a higher value of himself than he felt inside.

Juan lived with his thirty-six-year-old grandmother and several of her young children, offspring of a series of husbands and lovers. Juan's twenty-two-year-old mother would frequently come over to the house, but would not take any notice of her little boy or even speak to him. She, too, had been married several times, and Juan was the product of a marriage she was trying to forget.

"You remind me too much of your father," she had told Juan, "and I hate your father. I don't want anything to do with you because you look so much like him." She meant it. She would come over to the house and totally ignore the little boy—pretending he wasn't there. On several occasions she took the other children on outings. But not Juan.

"I wish I could go to the zoo," Juan told Kari later, "but my momma won't take me anywhere because she doesn't like me."

Kari determined she was going to treasure Juan every day—and do what she could to help his cut-and-pasted family.

Taking it upon herself to raise some money, she enlisted our family's help to move the grandmother's household out of a hovel in a high crime area into a neat-but-tiny, three-room apartment nearer Juan's school. We brought the family some furniture, which deeply touched their hearts.

As time went by, Juan's problems with fighting began to diminish. His classwork showed marked improvement. And he no longer fled from his nightly hug. For the first time in his life, Juan felt valued...and valuable.

Kari, an outsider, was doing for her class what moms and dads have the opportunity to do every day of the year. She was *treasuring* her children, and if we want light to shine in our homes down through the years, so must we.

How do you do this? What does it mean to "treasure" another

human being? Is it just so much flowery talk—or does it cut into the bone and sinew of life itself?

To treasure something means to attach great importance or high value to it. People take good care of what they treasure. Have you noticed it?

If your hobby is restoring classic cars, you probably don't let your teenager take them off-road to jump gullies in the desert. If you're a stamp-collector, you know how to pick up those precious little squares with special tweezers and ever-so-gently slip them into protective sleeves.

People take time with what they treasure. If you're a football fanatic, your Saturdays, Sundays, and Monday nights are sewed up from September through January. If you do decoupage, each piece of art takes twelve painstaking coats of shellac—with a twelve-hour drying period between each coat.

Based on the amount of care and time you invest in each activity, your family can sense what is truly important to you. If your children or spouse feel you are not as thoughtful and concerned about them as you are with your other interests and involvements, they will realize they are not as valuable to you, *no matter what you say.*

One of our friends told of being deeply enmeshed in a thick novel over a period of several days. He had thought he was giving "adequate time" to his children, but was startled back to reality when his first-grade daughter forcibly crawled up into his lap, pushed down the paperback, and said, "Which do you love most? Your book, or me?"

It's a valid question. *Which do you love most? What do you treasure?*

I (John) remember a time when I really needed to know I was valuable—treasured by someone—and words alone weren't enough.

I had just gotten engaged when I applied to a certain school to pursue doctoral studies. Throughout our courtship, the planning and dreaming about attending this out-of-state school filled our conversations. Cindy was so supportive and positive. Yes, she understood how much time I would have to spend studying, and yes, whatever sacrifices it took to get me though school she was willing to make. One day, however, in less than ten seconds, something happened that made all those sacrifices unnecessary.

For several months, the highlight of my day had been walking to the mailbox, looking for the acceptance letter I knew would come. Then one afternoon the letter finally arrived.

I had thought about what I'd do when I opened it. I thought about waiting until that night when Cindy and I could open it together. But the suspense was killing me so I ripped it open…and in less than three lines—three *mimeographed* lines—all my dreams were ripped apart as well.

I had been rejected for admission. I had failed to get into this school, and at that point my whole life seemed like a failure. Waves of embarrassment, anger, and confusion covered me. Why had I told so many people about my plans to attend this school? What now? And most of all, how would I face my new fiancée with the fact that she was engaged to a miserable failure instead of a doctoral student?

Somehow, Cindy had already learned of my not getting into school that day (bad news travels fast!). We had a date that evening, and I showed up so low I could have played handball against the curb. I was greeted, however, by a woman who knew then—and still knows today—how to make her man feel treasured.

Cindy had fixed a great dinner and let me pour out all my frustration and hurt. She didn't lecture, she didn't show her disappointment. What she did was to tell me that God could still use me, and that as far as she was concerned, I was already "Dr. Trent" to her—even if no school in the country would accept me.

She didn't hand me a diploma that night, but her gentle way of treasuring me in that major time of disappointment was like getting an honorary degree from Harvard. To my dry, downcast spirit, Cindy's actions and attitude were like Southern California getting a drenching rain after five years of drought. They gave me a new perspective, renewed hope, and a positive reminder that my value in Christ did not depend on a degree from any school.

Less than four months later, just before we were married, we were offered a wonderful job in a major city. And less than a year after that, I opened the mailbox to find an *acceptance* letter from a different school, not far from our new home, with an equally good program.

Our wives put into practice the skills of treasuring people. Unfortunately, we often meet creative businessmen and women who work only part-time at the priority of honoring others. These people make a great deal of money with their business skills by honoring their employees, and show a marked sensitivity and awareness of their needs. But many of these same men and women go home at night and fail to apply these principles to their spouses and families.

Without meaning to, a parent or spouse can communicate nonverbally that other people or activities are more important to him or her than family. You've heard of football widows. How about golf orphans?

A man recently told us how his five-year-old boy began to tear up every time dad opened the closet and reached for his clubs. The man finally realized he had wounded his son through a lack of attention. Every time he headed out the door to go golfing, it was like bumping up against a painful bruise.

To this man's credit, he took those tears seriously, and decided on a radical remedy. He vowed not to touch the clubs again until his boy was old enough to golf *with* him. And he has kept that vow. He made the decision to treasure his son more than a personal pastime that also meant a great deal to him. Today he can see the appreciation in his son's eyes when he makes room for him in his life on Saturdays. But how much more will that appreciation grow as that boy gets older, and realizes what his father gave up for him!

We recently talked with another man who told us, "When I was in high school, my father took a new job he really liked. When football season started, he would fly back every weekend to see my games—until his boss told him he couldn't do it anymore. So my father quit his job so that he could see his son play football. *I know that my father loved me, because I know what he gave up to spend time with me.*"

We're not saying that children will only feel valuable if we give up a favorite hobby or switch careers. The issue is simply this: With their fine-tuned radar system, a child picks up whether he is more valuable to you than your property or projects at work.

We would be the first to admit that it's easy to talk a good game here. It's easy to say we "value" our relationship with Christ. It's easy to affirm that our spouses or families are "important" or "precious" to us. We convince ourselves that this is true. But what does the record really show? Where are we *actually* investing the cream of our time and thoughts and energies? THAT is what we really treasure.

Treasuring is an attitude we carry in our hearts, a conviction we make deep inside. It is one big decision that plays itself out in ten thousand little decisions every day of our lives. Yet this one giant decision to treasure our loved ones lights up a home like nothing else in life.

*My wife wants to read me "something cute" from an article in a magazine...but I'm deep into my spy novel.*

*My little girl has skinned her knee and wants my attention NOW, but I've been waiting half an hour for the TV sports update that just started.*

*My boy wants to describe—in painstaking detail—his idea for an underwater helicopter, but I'm trying to set the table for dinner.*

*My teenager asks for help on a complicated social studies project, but I was already halfway out the door to go jogging—and I only have thirty minutes.*

All of us face these sorts of mini-dilemmas in the course of our day, and not one of them is really "a big deal" in itself. Yet little actions and replies and decisions weave a pattern over the days and weeks and years—and that pattern reveals the content of our hearts.

Treasuring is obeying God's value system. And we don't have to guess what that might be. Jesus stated it clearly when He said, "Love the Lord your God with all your heart and with all your soul and with all your mind.... Love your neighbor as yourself" (Matthew 22:37,39). These two commands cover all the commands of Scripture: to treasure God with all your heart and to treasure people, while you are valuing yourself.

"But I just can't remember to do those 'little things,' or even to tell my kids that I love them!" you might say. Yet the doing and saying come more naturally out of a basic decision to highly value them.

Notice the order here: God first, others second, myself third. That doesn't mean I'm a "low-level" person. But others—especially my family—are higher, and God is highest of all. Parents who ignore or disregard God's value system find trouble and inevitable heartache as their children grow up. For instance, an adolescent boy who has grown up with a deficient sense of value often tends to misuse and mistreat others. If he doesn't value God and doesn't see any value in himself, why should he value the girl he happens to be dating? *What do I care? I'll sleep with her and I won't think of the consequences. So she gets pregnant. Big deal. So she gets an abortion. That's her choice. So what? I'm not valuable, she's not valuable, life itself isn't that valuable, so why not have as much fun as I can?*

Let's say this same individual reaches his twenties, gets married, and has kids of his own. Does he value his wife? Does he value his family? *Hey, I'm not going to worry about taking time with my wife. I'm not going to pour my life into these kids. I'm going out with the guys. I'm going to play with my toys.*

In our counseling, we've heard of this kind of pattern repeated generation after generation. It was true with both of our fathers growing up. My (John's) father was an angry ex-marine who walked out on his family when we were young. Gary's father carried a full load of bitterness over the way *he* had been raised, constantly exploding in anger and devaluing his kids.

Both of us have had to cry out to God for help in breaking negative patterns, and have had to say over and over, "By God's grace I'm going to stop this pattern right here. By God's grace, I'm going to leave the light on in my home."

Two new generations of kids are being raised today who have learned to treasure others—because they've felt what it's like to be a treasure themselves.

How then, can we as parents begin to treasure our children in a way that will teach them to value others? Here are a few suggestions to help you begin a lifelong journey.

*1. Tell them how valuable they are to you!*

It's so simple. So obvious. You assume they already know it. But don't assume anything! Like an electric circuit with a break in the line, never telling a child he's valuable fails to close the loop and free the current that lights the bulb. Until you complete the circuit with your words, the light of unconditional love will never shine in a child's life.

I (John) know of one woman who longed to hear her father's words of love and acceptance. Finally, she sent a letter to her father, asking him if he would write and tell her he loved her. Actually, he did far better than that. In a short time, she received a cassette tape—nearly *two hours* in length—that told story after story about how he loved and appreciated her.

He closed the tape (and closed the circuit) by asking her forgiveness that he had never been able to say to her in person those things he had hid in his heart for years. Yet in the safety of his own room with a tape recorder, he was finally able to put into words the blessing she longed for so much.

Why is it that we are so reluctant to tell our children how valuable they are to us? We need to let them know regularly that they are tremendously important to us. On a scale of one-to-ten, where do your children feel they rate in importance to you? Have your ever *asked* them? Are you prepared for how they might answer?

In Don's home, there was never any doubt. Don, a godly man in my (John's) home church made a life-long commitment to verbally express love to his children. From the time his two daughters and son were babies, he would sing them a Swedish lullaby every night in his strong, heavily accented voice. That well-worn love song floated through their bedrooms at night when he put them to bed...and then through the years in their memories as the children grew up and left home. Even though the children didn't understand a word of Swedish, his love translated loud and clear in their hearts.

This past March, he sang that song to his children yet again. Only this time, in a weak, cracking voice, at a local hospice where he lay dying. It was one last attempt to cheer up his now grown children who had gathered at his bedside. To let them know he loved them. To verbalize the light of love would never go out, even when the light in his eyes grew dim.

As you make your expressions of love and value in your home, make sure they are not linked solely to your child's *performance* on a task.

When statements of value are only linked to a child's accomplishments, the words lose much of their impact. Children who have to "perform" to get a parental blessing retain a nagging uncertainty about whether they really received it. If their performance ever drops even a small amount, they might wonder, *Am I loved for "who I am" or only for "what I can do"?*

*2. Make an unconditional commitment to them for life.*

That's the kind of commitment that says, "You're important to me today and tomorrow, no matter what happens—no matter what the cost."

At a conference we did recently, I (John) heard a powerful story of a woman who grew up in a home where the father knew how to communicate unconditional love.

"From the time I was five years old," the woman told us, "I wanted to be a teacher. My father was a farmer, and we were always very tight on money. But he and mother scrimped and saved for years—even during the depression—so that I would have enough money to go to college.

"I did graduate and taught for one year, but then I got married, quit teaching, and within a year had our first child. Four other children followed. Then something happened that I will never forget.

"After the birth of my fifth child, I overheard a neighbor ask my father, 'Are you sorry now you sacrificed so much to send your daughter to college?' My father answered him by saying he had no regrets at all, and that he was sure that all I had learned in school would be useful to me, my family, and others one day.

"I stayed home until my children were much older, but ultimately I did go back into teaching and taught high school—*for thirty years!*"

Treasuring a child will often mean sacrifice, but if those sacrifices are given with a "no regrets" attitude, the result can bless entire generations.

We make it a point to tell our children that we love them and are committed to them for their entire lives, no matter what they do. We are committed to help them be successful in whatever they want to do. We will be committed to them after they are married. We will be committed to them no matter whom they marry. We will be committed to them no matter what happens during their marriage. We will be committed to their mates and to their children. We will always be available to listen. Should they get into trouble, we will be there to help. That doesn't necessarily mean we will bail them out of a tight situation, for that may not be best for them. But they know how much we love them and that nothing can ever keep us from loving them.

*3. Schedule special times with the family.*

Communicating warm, loving approval to our children doesn't "just happen" naturally. We believe this time should be scheduled regularly—preferably several times each week—because our children need us.

In counseling, we often talk about the fact that children have little "love tanks." Some days, they may come home from school and need a complete fill-up. On other days, they just need a little affirmation to top off their tanks. Let their tanks run dry too long, however, and they'll close their spirit and often react in anger and distance themselves from us. Consistent, meaningful contact that fills their tanks with love is crucial. That may take fifteen minutes of listening about their day, giving them a word of praise, asking them to tell you their dreams or fears, or learning about their favorite hobby or sport. The activity itself is not so important, but it does need to be something enjoyable for both the child and the parent.

Have you ever taken your son or daughter out for breakfast...just the two of you?

Have you ever gone for a walk with your teenager on a starry night?

Have you ever made Christmas decorations as a family?

Often the deepest relationships can be developed during the simplest activities.

Camping, hiking, and outdoor activity provide prime opportunities to bond with our families. Sitting around a campfire, walking along a mountain trail, or waiting by a lakeside for the fish to bite offer never-to-be-duplicated moments to talk on a deeper level with our children. These special times help us understand where they are going in life and what concerns them. Just being *with them* communicates they are loved. A parent's willingness to wait for conversation to develop further amplifies their child's self-worth.

*4. Communicate that you are available to your children, both during scheduled and unscheduled times.*

Here's where real life pokes its head into the cloudy world of our good intentions and says, "Are you for real?" We're reading our new *Time* magazine, watching something special on TV, or heading out the door for a meeting, and one of our children walks up and says, "Dad, do you have a minute? I have this problem in Algebra," or, "Mom, what am I going to do? I can't find anything to wear." We must be careful what we communicate at these times. If we say, "Uh, sure, in a few minutes," or, "Not now, I'm busy," kids will observe *what* we are doing and compare their own importance to it.

We can say, "Now isn't a good time to talk, but I can give you my undivided attention within thirty minutes, guaranteed." That's okay (if we follow through!), but it will say even more if we drop what we're doing, because our children are simply more important.

*5. Make yourself accountable to a friend or a small group to follow through in this crucial matter of treasuring.*

No one said this would be easy! Important life decisions seldom are. But if this determination to treasure your family is going to be more than a nice, passing thought, make it a point to register your decision with some folks who will walk the first few miles of that long road with you...and firmly remind you (in love) to stay the course if you try to turn back!

Your home may never have all the goodies, gadgets, and material "treasures" you've wished for and wanted over the years. Your residence may never make the pages of *House Beautiful,* and your story may never be told on "The Lifestyles of the Rich and Famous." But have no doubt: there is treasure, real treasure, in the homes of those who turn against the current of popular culture and determine to place high value on God and their family.

Whether your home is large or small, it's a home your children will always return to in their memories...if you remember to leave the light on.

"Be devoted to one another in brotherly love, giving preference to one another in honor" (Romans 12:10, NASB).

# Chapter Two

# THE PRICELESS VALUE OF AFFIRMATION

Sixth grade hadn't been a banner year for Eric. Never very confident in school, he had a particular dread of mathematics. "A mental block," one of the school counselors had told him. Then, as if a mental math block wasn't enough for an eleven-year-old kid to deal with, he came down with measles in the fall and had to stay out of school for two weeks. By the time he got back, his classmates were *multiplying* fractions. Eric was still trying to figure out what you get when you put a half a pie with three-quarters of a pie…besides a lot of pie.

Eric's teacher, Mrs. Gunther—loud, overweight, terrifying, and a year away from retirement—was unsympathetic. For the rest of the year she called him "Measly" in honor of his untimely spots and hounded him with ceaseless makeup assignments. When his mental block prevented his progress in fractions, she would thunder at him in front of the class, "I don't give a Continental for your excuses! You'd better straighten up, Measly. Them ain't wings I hear flappin'!"

The mental block, once the size of a backyard fence, now loomed like the Great Wall of China. Eric despaired of ever catching up, and even fell behind in subjects he'd been good at.

When he began seventh grade, he found himself in all the "slow-learner" classes. No one expected Eric to be bright or successful—least of all Eric.

Then came a remarkable Moment.

It happened in the middle of Mrs. Warwick's ninth grade English class. To this day, some twenty-five years later, Eric still lights up as he recalls the Moment.

The fifth period class had been yawning through Mrs. Warwick's attempts to spark discussion about a Mark Twain short story. At some point in the lecture, something clicked in Eric's mind. It was probably crazy, but it suddenly seemed like he understood something Twain had been driving at—something a little below the surface. Despite himself, Eric raised his hand and ventured an observation.

That led to the Moment when Mrs. Warwick looked straight into Eric's eyes, beamed with pleasure, and said, "Why, Eric…that was *very* perceptive of you!"

Perceptive. Perceptive? Perceptive!

The word echoed in Eric's thoughts for the rest of the day—and then for the rest of his life. *Perceptive? Me? Well, yeah. I guess that WAS perceptive. Maybe I AM perceptive.*

One word, one little positive word dropped at the right moment somehow tipped the balance in a teenager's view of himself—and possibly changed the course of his life. (Even though he still can't multiply fractions.)

Eric went on to pursue a career in journalism and eventually became a book editor, working successfully with some of the top authors in America.

Many teachers are well aware how praise motivates children. One teacher said she praised each student in her third grade class every day, without exception. Her students were the most motivated, encouraged, and enthusiastic in the school. I (Gary) remember what happened when my high school geometry teacher began to affirm me regularly. Within six weeks my D average climbed to an A.

It's wonderful when a teacher has the opportunity to inject a word of affirmation into a child's life. But after years of counseling, we have concluded that the most powerful form of affirmation takes place at home, and if withheld, can leave a lasting scar in a child's life.

### "LONGER, DADDY, LONGER..."

Recently, a woman grabbed my arm at a conference after I (John) had finished speaking on the enormous need we all have for affirmation.

"Dr. Trent, may I tell you my story?" she asked. "Actually, it's a story of something my son did with my granddaughter that illustrates what you've been talking about—the importance of affirmation.

"My son has two daughters, one who's five and one who is in the 'terrible twos.'" When a *grandmother* says this child is in the "terrible twos," *believe me*, she is!

"For several years, my son has taken the oldest girl out for a 'date' time, but he had never taken the two-year-old until recently. On his first 'date' with the younger one, he took her out for breakfast at a local fast food restaurant.

"They had just gotten their pancakes and my son decided it would be a good time to tell this child how much he loved and appreciated her."

"Jenny," her son had said, "I want you to know how much I love you, and how special you are to Mom and me. We prayed for you for years, and now that you're here and growing up to be such a wonderful girl, we couldn't be more proud of you."

Once he had said all this, he stopped talking and reached over for his fork to begin eating...but he never got the fork to his mouth.

His daughter reached out her little hand and laid it on her father's hand. His eyes went to hers, and in a soft, pleading voice she said, *"Longer, Daddy...longer."*

He put his fork down and proceeded to tell her some more reasons and ways they loved and appreciated her, and then he again reached for his fork. A second time...and a third...*and a fourth* time he heard the words, "Longer, Daddy...longer."

This father never did get much to eat that morning, but his daughter got the emotional nourishment she needed so much. In fact, a few days later, she spontaneously ran up to her mother and said, "I'm a really special daughter, Mommy. Daddy told me so."

Words have awesome power to build us up or tear us down emotionally. This is particularly true within the family. Many people can clearly remember words of praise their parents spoke years ago. Others can remember negative, cutting words—with the whole scene etched in extraordinary detail on their minds.

Affirming words from moms and dads are like light switches. Speak a word of affirmation at the right moment in a child's life and it's like lighting up a whole roomful of possibilities.

*My, you're a good helper, Tommy. You know, you're just a fun little guy to have around! You brighten up our whole family.*

*I can't believe the colors you used in that picture, Sarah! See how they blend together here? You really have a good eye for color.*

*Ken, that was just your second soccer game, but I was really impressed by the way you seemed to sense where the ball was going. Not everyone can do that kind of thing. I sure couldn't do it when I was a boy. I'll bet you're really going to be good at this game.*

*Was that you singing just then, Jean? You're kidding! Boy, you have a pretty voice. I hope you think about choir as you get older.*

Unfortunately, negative words—or just the lack of affirming ones—can turn out the lights in a child's life. Lights that may never be lit again.

Solomon wrote, "A man finds joy in giving an apt reply—and how good is a timely word!" (Proverbs 15:23). And again, "A word aptly spoken is like apples of gold in settings of silver" (Proverbs 25:11).

Few of us really understand or appreciate the sheer power of words. The book of James, however, uses several startling word pictures to help us grasp that force. First, James pictures our tongue as a "bit" used to direct a horse (James 3:3). If you control a horse's mouth by means of a small bit, the entire animal will move in the direction you choose. The second picture portrays this same principle in a different way. Here a "small rudder" is used to turn a mighty ship in the midst of the sea (3:4). These analogies highlight the way spoken words can direct and control a person or a relationship.

A mom, dad, aunt, uncle, or friend can use this power of the tongue for good. He or she can steer a child away from trouble or provide guidance to a friend making an important decision. He or she can minister words of encouragement or plant seeds of praise that can grow into mighty trees—like pillars that uphold an entire life.

*Even the smallest act of affirmation can bring large benefits to a child.* How tiny those seeds can be! A woman we know had a very poor self image as a junior higher. Because of several childhood illnesses, she was pale, thin, and underdeveloped for her age. An alert pastor's wife, however, found something to compliment. Stopping the girl in church one Sunday, the woman said, "Teri, you look so good with that red hairband. I think red really compliments you!"

The comment only took a few seconds and is now decades in the past. The junior high girl is now a wife and mother. Yet if you would look in her closet, you would immediately see a predominance of red. She has felt good about herself wearing that color ever since.

Opportunities to affirm are varied, but it takes an awake, perceptive parent to maximize the moment. Kids look to their parents to put the events of their lives—the ups and downs—in context. Mom or Dad have the opportunity to *frame* and give meaning to such occurrences. It takes a loving, attentive parent to take a common stone and make it into a *milestone* in a son or daughter's life.

This might be particularly true in the teenage years. At the tender age of sixteen, everything in life seems somehow magnified. The smallest setback or put-down can be devastating. The most insignificant slip or failure can be terminally embarrassing. At the same time, the least bit of encouragement—from the right person at the right moment—can become hugely significant.

Boys and girls in their midteens are standing on a tightrope between childhood and adulthood—and something always seems to be shaking one end of the rope or the other.

A number of years ago, I (Gary) watched my youngest son out on that shaky tightrope—and frankly wondered how he was going to do. Through his sophomore year in high school, Michael's principle desire seemed to be remaining *invisible*. His grades were so-so. He was content to stay in the background of things. He played several sports, but never seemed inclined to excel. His motto seemed to be, "Just make it through."

Then, the summer before his junior year, something amazing happened that dramatically changed that attitude right in front of our eyes. At Kannakuk Camp in Branson, Missouri (what we feel is the top Christian sports camp in the country), Michael was elected "Chief" of his high school camp, after being one of five nominees in a group numbering over three hundred.

Before the announcement, he was beside himself with excitement at his nomination, yet he always added in every conversation, "Yeah, I know I won't win."

Yet win he did—the first time he had ever won anything in his life. He was stunned! It was unquestionably one of the greatest days of his life. But when I think about it now, how easy it would have been for Norma and me, vacationing in a cabin near the camp, to have minimized or overlooked that moment in our son's life. I might have said...

*"Huh? Oh, yeah, that's great, Mike. Boy, did you see that eagle flying over the lake this morning? Did you see the size of that thing? It must have been..."*

*"Chief? Hey, way-to-go. Norm, did you want to go into Branson and do some shopping this afternoon?"*

*"Well, let's not get too carried away, Michael. This is just camp, remember? Now if you'd just apply yourself a little harder in school you might..."*

Michael looked to us to *interpret* that honor by his peers. To put a frame around that day in his life. Was it a big deal, or wasn't it? Did it really say something about his potential, or didn't it? We could have easily—and inadvertently—destroyed that moment by preoccupation with other things. Instead of turning on a light in his life, we could have put that light out, perhaps for the rest of his life.

But after missing too many other opportunities to affirm my kids, I was determined not to miss this one. I almost came unglued, I got so excited about it. We all hugged him, congratulating him endlessly. One of our dear friends, Jim Shaughnessy, pitched in and said, "Great, Mike! Nothing that big has ever happened to me!"

The very next day I went to a local wood artist and had him carve a large plaque with an Indian head on it. I bought some paints and painted the feathers of the headdress, and then inscribed the plaque with a message.

CHIEF SMALLEY
Kannakuk Camp
Summer 1988

For the next several years that plaque hung in a prominent place in Michael's bedroom.

But something happened that summer that was more significant than a memento on a wall. The change in my son's life was staggering. You could almost see him say to himself, *Maybe I am capable. Maybe I can accomplish some things.*

He went on to become student body president of his high school, played on championship varsity basketball and football teams, was elected homecoming king, and got serious about his grades and about preparing for the university. This domino reaction all started with that first "little" domino at camp...an ordinary stone along the path that became a milestone.

As a parent, you have the awesome opportunity to immortalize moments in your child's life. One of our friends recently told us—almost in tears—that his folks never went to a single one of his ballgames or activities when he was a boy. To this day he remembers standing on a riser in his choir robe in front of a huge audience as part of a select all-state youth choir, yet feeling no joy or excitement at all. His heart felt like a lump of lead in his chest because his mom and dad, both white-collar professionals, weren't in that audience. Neither "had time" to come.

An incident that could have been carefully framed and honored for a lifetime was thrown away. The memory brings our friend no pleasure, because his parents had given it no value.

We need to look for even the smallest of opportunities to affirm our kids, mate, or friends—*while carefully controlling our criticisms.*

This is particularly true for those who are fond of saying, "I'm not criticizing you.... I'm just criticizing your behavior." For too many people, who they are and what they do are so closely connected that to hammer one is to smash the other.

Another friend told us about "inspecting" his six-year-old daughter's job of cleaning the family room. She had really worked hard on it and her eyes were dancing with expectation as she took her dad's hand and led him to the room.

Our friend had really meant to affirm her, and yet the first words out of his mouth were, "Well, it's not *perfect*, but..." He described how her face fell in an instant and she began to weep. Her joy over what she considered a "job well done" evaporated just that fast.

How quick we are to pick out one negative while ignoring five equally obvious positives!

*"Yeah, you went three for four in that game, but you could have made that last hit. I think it's your stance at the plate. If you'd just..."*

*"You combed your hair all by yourself this morning? I can tell. There's a cowlick standing straight up in the back!"*

Unless we parents are careful, our body language and facial expressions will tend to minimize our praise while maximizing the critique.

Here are several suggestions for building affirmation into the life of your family. Practice these things and light will begin to radiate from the windows of your home...and the eyes of those you love.

*1. Make it your goal to praise each child at least once a day for something.*

A parent has to be on the hunt for things to affirm. You are panning for gold—looking for a tiny, gleaming fleck in a panful of gray rocks and ordinary sand. When you find that grain of gold, let yourself go a little. "Gold! Hey, look at this! I've found *gold!*"

Bedtime is a good moment to review your goal of praising each child. If upon review you realize you've had nothing positive to say all day long, take time to say it then!

Cindy and I (John) often sit on our daughter's bed and use the last few minutes of the evening to pour one more cup of affirmation onto our little one's life. The first and last ten minutes of the day are so crucial. Imagine waking up and going to bed every night feeling loved and valued! There's nothing like sending a little boy or girl off to dreamland with warm words of parental praise ringing in their ears—and having them wake up to the same tune.

*2. "Sandwich" all your criticism between words of affirmation.*

Should you criticize at all? Yes, of course, but even this can become an affirming experience. We try to use the "sandwich approach" with our kids. The "meat" is the criticism and the "bun" on both sides is the praise. Make the bun three feet thick!

In *The Sixty Second Father*, the author talks about getting firm with his son for thirty seconds, and then holding him for the next thirty seconds, making sure the last verbal emphasis is nothing but solid praise and admiration.

*3. Be specific with your praise.*

*Specific* praise is far more effective than *general* praise. Tousling a child's hair and saying, "You're a great kid," might be appreciated, but probably won't be remembered. Take the time to cite particular things. (This requires keeping your eyes open!)

*"You've sure been a loyal friend to Michelle. It's easy to drop friends or forget about them when you've had an argument or other kids come around. But you've really stuck with her. That says something to me about your character—something I'm very proud of."*

*"I noticed the way you gave your little sister that toy out of the Cheerios box—even though she got the sticker from Raisin Bran last week. That was very generous of you—and I'm sure it was pleasing to the Lord."*

Both the Smalleys and Trents often use word pictures to communicate in a tangible way a specific characteristic being singled out for praise.

For example, a few years ago, I (John) was on the road for a publicity tour over Valentine's Day. Now, don't feel too badly for Cindy. She got a special dinner before I left on the trip, flowers and cards on that day, and a second Valentine's celebration when I returned. Yet of all the things I did to express love to my wife, one thing stood out to her.

Before we left, I gave Cindy a clothespin—just a standard, wooden, five-cent clothespin—along with the heartfelt words, "Honey, you do such a great job of holding the whole family together with all our busy schedules—I want you to have this clothespin."

When I came home, there was the clothespin I'd given her. Only now it had become a lasting memory of those few words I'd shared. While I was gone, she had glued a magnet to the back, drawn a red heart on the front, and put it on a prominent place on the refrigerator! (Remember: If you want to know what is really important to a person, just look at their refrigerator door!)

*4. Don't be surprised if the smallest act of affirmation has long-reaching effects.*

The year was 1952, and for my (John's) mother, it was a year of heartache, pain, and transition. There were no displaced homemaker programs in the 1950s, and with three children under three (that happens when you have a two-year-old and twins!), my mother had suddenly become a single parent when my father walked out.

There would be no child support. No alimony or family money to soften the blow. And without a college degree or any workplace experience, Mom was suddenly forced to balance time and care for us with a part-time job and her one ticket upward—business school.

I'm proud to say that my mother did graduate from business school, and go on to have a wonderful career in the banking business. In fact, she became so accomplished that she was the first businesswoman to ever grace the cover of the *Wall Street Journal*, back in 1959. But by her own account, none of that would have happened if it hadn't been for one word of encouragement from a woman whose name she can't even remember.

During those early days of business school, she struggled with typing—and with her typing teacher. Recently retired from the Army, he grilled and drilled his students with anything but kid gloves. And he seemed to particularly pick on my mother.

He would pull out the wadded up pieces of paper, filled with errors, that filled the trash can near where my mother sat. Then he'd roar at her that she'd *never* be a good typist at the rate she was going. With all the pressures of work and home she was under, and with typing being a required part of her curriculum, an outburst at the end of one class session left her weeping. As the students filed out of class, Mom just put her head down on the desk and cried. That's when a schoolmate stepped in with a brief word of encouragement.

"Honey," came a soft, southern voice.

Mom looked up at a round, pretty face with both tenderness and a glint of steel shining through brown eyes.

"Honey, you just hang in there, ya here? You're gonna make it—I *know* you will. And startin' tomorrow, you just *fold* those papers you're throwin' away before you put 'em in the waste basket. That way they don't stack up so much, and he won't bother you so much."

With that she was gone, but her words of encouragement and hope gave my mom the courage to come in the next day with the feeling, *Maybe I can make it.* With that renewed hope (and now folding each paper she threw away), Mom earned her teacher's first backhanded compliment.

After inspecting her waste basket, he muttered, "I guess Zoa is finally getting with things."

The years fly by so quickly, don't they? Opportunities to drop seeds of affirmation into the heart of a child or a spouse—or even a discouraged classmate—may not be as numerous as we might imagine. Let's set aside some of our many "important" distractions and make sure this great good gets done in our homes...even today.

The apostle Paul probably said it best: "Do not let any unwholesome talk come out of your mouths, but only what is helpful for *building others up* according to their needs, that it may benefit those who listen.... Be very careful, then, how you live—not as unwise but as wise, making the most of every opportunity, because the days are evil" (Ephesians 4:29, 5:15-16).

Paul knew how to leave the lights on.

# MEANINGFUL TOUCH

T he young GI stepped into line with the other teenagers to get his barbecued chicken. It's funny how some people can look eighteen—until you look at their eyes. I think it was his haunted look that caused me to notice him that evening. From the window of his eyes, he looked like a tired old man, not like the swarm of happy kids around him.

I (John) was part of a work crew at Trail West, Young Life's beautiful camp high in the Colorado Rockies. It was my job that night to stand at the head of the line and hand out the best smelling, best tasting barbecued chicken I'd ever eaten—before or since.

We had our huge grill fired up in the middle of a large, grassy meadow, rimmed by massive, solemn pines that stood like a majestic fence around us. The sun was sliding behind the surrounding mountain peaks as the fragrant smoke from our barbecue drifted across the clearing.

It was 1969, the summer of my junior year of high school. It didn't occur to me then, but while the laughing, noisy high schoolers waited for their meal that evening, a number of their dads, friends, schoolmates, and older brothers were fighting and dying in the rice paddies and jungles of Southeast Asia.

It was easy to spot the young 'Nam vet in our midst. In an era of sideburns and shaggy haircuts, his government-issue "buzz-cut" drew plenty of sidelong glances. He had actually graduated from high school a couple of years before, but his parents had gotten special permission for him to attend the camp.

That's the kind of crazy war it was: Two weeks before, he'd been fighting for his life, watching buddies drop all around him. Then suddenly his tour was up, he was airlifted out of a fierce firefight to Saigon, got on a commercial airliner, and headed home. Just like that.

Now he was on leave, standing in line in a Rocky Mountain meadow with a bunch of kids who didn't seem to have a care in the world.

I first noticed him when he was about the fourth person from the front of the line. His face was extremely pale and he was visibly trembling. I remember thinking, *Something's wrong with this guy. He must be getting sick.*

As he got closer to the grill, he began shaking even harder. I picked up a piece of chicken with my tongs and was just about to serve him when he suddenly dropped his plate, spilling beans and salad on the ground and on the person in front of him. With a choked cry, he took off on a dead run for the forest.

Everyone stopped talking and just stared. We all wondered, *What in the world's with him?*

Our Young Life leader headed off after the young soldier, and after they both disappeared into the trees, the dinner line resumed its onward march.

Doug found him hiding in the trees, shaking like a leaf. The older man, a burly ex-football player, towered nearly a foot above the soldier and probably outweighed him by a hundred pounds. But without saying a word, he gently put his arms around the trembling camper and held him tight.

The young soldier buried his face in our leader's chest and sobbed uncontrollably. They stood together in the twilight for nearly twenty minutes. The young man sobbing, the older man holding him, saying nothing.

When he finally was able to compose himself, they sat on a log together and the vet tried to explain what was going on.

Over in 'Nam, he said, if you were out in open country like that, with so many people milling around, you could expect the mortar rounds to start coming in. He had seen his sergeant killed, right in front of him, by an incoming shell. And no matter how hard he tried, he couldn't keep the sights and sounds from coming back.

Just before he reached the head of the line, it was as if he could hear the whistle of artillery fire and the screams of "Incoming! Incoming!" He couldn't take it any longer and ran to find cover.

That was day two of the camp, of what would become the most important week of this young man's life. Before the week was over, the soldier surrendered his life to a new Commander, Jesus Christ. But not for the reason you may think.

On the final night of camp, as we all sat around a big bonfire, campers were encouraged to stand up and make public their confession of faith if they had come to know Christ that week. Many young men and women responded to the opportunity, citing talks by the speaker, the encouragement of a close friend from home, and other causes as reasons for coming to know Jesus personally. The young soldier was one of the last to stand.

His story was much different from the rest. He began by telling how skeptical he had been about coming to camp. In fact, the only reason he agreed to come was that his parents promised to buy him a used car. The thought of his own wheels pushed him over the edge, and he came reluctantly to camp.

While everyone had been "real nice" to him, it wasn't a special friendship that had shaped his decision. Even though he thought the speaker had some good words to say, and made the gospel clear, it wasn't because of him either that he was responding to Christ.

What had really broken through to him was "that big guy," Doug, who had been willing to stand there in the trees with him and hold him until a piece of nightmare loosened its grip. In short, God used a hug—not a lecture, not a long walk through the trees, not a testimony—to win the bigger spiritual battle he was fighting.

## THE POWER OF TOUCH

We consistently underestimate it. Undersell it. Undervalue it. Underuse it. Yet touch has the power to instantly calm, reassure, transfer courage, and stabilize a situation beginning to spin out of control. To the degree that we choose to employ it in our family relationships, we will push back the threatening shadows of anger, bitterness, loneliness, and insecurity.

Whether a person is struggling mentally, emotionally, spiritually, or physically, a tender touch has the capacity to bring calmness and healing. But touch is also very important to communicate concern, love, and value during the quieter seasons of life. Medical studies show that men who meaningfully hug and touch others are actually more healthy and live longer than those who do not!

Everyone needs to be touched. We believe God not only ordained and mandated it, He *modeled* it in Christ. Husbands and wives need to decide they will regularly hold, touch, and caress each other.

Dads need to make sure they are holding their children regularly, reading to them, and taking walks where holding hands or an arm around the shoulder is as natural as taking the next step. Both moms and dads should look for ten to twenty opportunities every day to extend physical contact to their children. It creates closeness, cements a sense of belonging and security, and is a major factor in family health.

Many parents don't realize it, but every child has a touch "bank," and to the degree we maintain a healthy balance in that account, we are helping them to resist immoral relationships and a host of other harmful substitutes for the parental tenderness they crave.

We recently heard a moving story of a little seven-year-old boy who pictures to an extreme the deep need every child has to be held and meaningfully touched.

Brian was the last of seven children. When he was only four, his father deserted the family and left the mother as the sole support. To put bread on the table for seven hungry mouths, Brian's mother had to take on two jobs—and get even less sleep than before. Brian adapted to his mother's new schedule as best he could, relying on the other children to care for most of his needs. But there was something that would fill his thoughts from the time his mother left early in the morning to the time she came home late at night.

"Mommy," he'd cry when he saw her. "Hold me! Hold me!"

Exhausted by her grueling days and overloaded by the pressures of trying to keep the family together, the last thing this mother wanted was a four-year-old jumping into her arms when she got home. In no uncertain terms, she would push him aside, always explaining that she just "needed some time and space" before interacting with the children.

Perhaps an adult could understand why she needed her "space." But denying this little boy his deep need for meaningful touch was like pushing him away from the only source of heat in the home on a cold, winter night.

In a desperate attempt to bring some kind of security and closeness to his life, little Brian would wander into his mother's room at night, before she came home. Often, he would take one of her blouses or undergarments to bed with him. Holding on to her clothing and having her smell around him was the only thing that could stop his tears and help him fall off into sleep. As a seven-year-old, struggling in his studies, Brian had taken a piece of his mother's clothing to school with him, again to give him that reassurance he missed along with his mother's touch. But when it fell out of his shirt during recess, a compassionate teacher uncovered the real reason behind him bringing it, and got Brian and his family some much needed help.

Brian's story isn't an isolated one. Studies on touch deprivation prove that infants and children can actually sicken and die from the lack of touch. An incident that came to our attention very recently confirmed our convictions about this crucial aspect of my (John's) family bonding.

## WHEN TOUCH IS WITHHELD

The young woman's story seemed all too familiar. She had to do some fast growing up when three major events converged at almost the same time: graduation from high school, a positive outcome on a pregnancy test, and a quick eviction notice from her parents.

The next step was also too familiar. The boyfriend who had impregnated her and spoken with such tenderness suddenly decided he "no longer loved her" and joined the Navy.

Before she could begin to get oriented to the bewildering pace of life change, she found herself with a baby, living in a one-bedroom shack, and working enough hours at a convenience store to pay the rent, hire a baby-sitter, and put food on the table.

Since there was no one else to be angry with, she became angry with her child—the baby boy with blonde hair so like his father. She was never abusive to him. She never screamed at him and always kept him diapered and fed. She simply decided she wasn't going to touch him. When he cried, she gave him no comfort. When he woke up from a nap, she gave him no smile. For this little boy, there were no pats, no cuddles, no tickles, no hand-holding, no kisses. Life had been cold to her; she was going to be cold right back.

By the time the boy was four, he had come to associate any touch at all with the fear of anger and discipline. When he misbehaved, he was spanked. That was the only kind of "touch" he knew.

The teacher of the four-year-olds' class knew she had a significant problem within five minutes of this boy's first day in Sunday school. To put it kindly, he was a terror. This wise teacher looked beyond the little boy's behavior and sat down with his mother the next day. Gently yet firmly, she urged the young mother to talk to their church counselor. After first helping her to see her need of a Savior, this counselor put into her hands a book we recently revised and updated, called *The Gift of the Blessing*.[1]

She read the pages hungrily and very quickly came to two crushing realizations. First, she realized that one major reason she had so hungered for intimacy with her boyfriend was that neither her mother or father had touched her or shown any physical tenderness while she was growing up. The second thing she realized was that she was doing the very same thing to her son.

Those realizations brought deep conviction. Suddenly it all seemed clear and she broke down in the counselor's office and wept. Maybe it wasn't too late. Her boy was only four. She couldn't recapture the days that had slipped by...but she could make a new beginning. She decided to make a change that very day by giving her son a big hug.

This change of heart made a deep impression on her boy. In fact, it nearly scared him to death.

"Come here," she said to him when he came out of the Sunday school room, "Mommy wants to give you a big hug." The little boy's eyes went very wide and then he took off like a shot. He probably thought, *It's a trick. She's going to catch me and then smack me one.* The more she tried to catch him and hold him, the more hysterical he became.

It took time. A long time. Over and over she would say, "Now honey, I want to give you a hug—just because I love you." Just as frequently he would scream, run away, cry, or try to fight his way out of her arms. Then came the day when he looked at her from across the room, smiled shyly, ran into her arms, and gave *her* a hug. That was the breakthrough in this new relationship between a mom who was learning how to touch with tenderness...and a little boy who was learning how to drink it in.

Later she would laugh and tell her counselor, "I need those hugs as much as he does!" They were both on their way to recovery.

But is touch really that powerful in a person's life?

Recently, I (John) met a medical doctor at one of the seminars I do around the country on the Old Testament concept of "The Blessing." After I had stressed the importance of appropriate, meaningful touch, this man told me his story. Even though he knows all about psychology, it took a lesson from a veteran nurse to show him how intensely touch can affect the lives of men, women, and babies!

This cardiologist and his wife had just had their first child—a precious, premature daughter who tipped the scales at just under three pounds. Like most doctors, he knew all too well the many complications and problems that his daughter potentially faced. As she lay hooked up to numerous monitors, it made him reluctant to touch her in her intensive care incubator.

Finally, on the second day, the head nurse of some twenty years, told him, "Look, Doctor. Your child needs you to *touch* her. You just reach your hand in that crib and touch her. And when you do, look at what happens to the monitors."

Reluctantly, he did so, and as he began to stroke the newborn's tiny arms and legs, the blood, oxygen, and chemical levels began to change noticeably—and then dramatically. This doctor could read those monitors, and before his eyes he could see the positive changes taking place in her little life through those small acts of touch.

It's no accident that premature babies who are touched and held as a regular part of their hospital stay gain weight some *47 percent faster* than those who are not. And it was no accident that this grateful father dates his strong emotional bond with his daughter from that day in the hospital nursery.

### TENDERNESS UNDER TRIAL

As my children have grown, I (Gary) have seen the fruit of consistent tenderness in their lives. My family is used to being hugged. Sometimes my twenty-four-year-old Kari will grab her brother Michael, nineteen, and give him a big kiss. Mike puts up a big front and mimics a little bush being sprayed with insecticide. But he loves it and even expects it. We've *trained* our kids to expect it. It's so normal and natural they don't feel awkward about it. My boys can hug me in any context.

I was at Michael's high school campus a couple of years ago speaking to a class and happened to bump into Mike in the hall with a group of his friends. He threw his arms around me and gave me a big hug. Rather than being embarrassed or scornful, it was obvious that several of his friends were envious of that sort of relationship.

When my kids come into contact with friends at school and camps who never get hugged in their homes, they're always encouraging me to "go talk to the parents." What they've experienced in their home life seems normal. The absence of that kind of tenderness seems *abnormal.*

Don't imagine that all of this has come easily or naturally to me! I came from a non-touching home and can't remember being hugged by my dad. Even after I became a Christian and learned that a soft answer turns away anger (Proverbs 15:1) and that a key fruit of the Spirit is "gentleness" (Galatians 5:23), I had never applied either principle in my most important relationships.

Since I wasn't fortunate enough to have a father who knew how to be tender to his wife, I wasn't aware that softness and meaningful touch during stressful times was even an option until several years into my marriage. That's when I became aware that one of a person's greatest needs is to be comforted, especially during those moments when life seems to be unraveling.

We pray you won't withhold this important aspect of honor from a child the way Jan's father did. When Jan was twelve and had just moved to a new school, she felt lost and confused.

"My need for my dad to hug me and tell me everything was going to be all right was so strong during this time, I actually jumped into his lap one night like I was a little kid.

" 'Get off me!' he screamed, and threw me off onto the floor. I landed flat on my back, and he shouted at me, 'Don't you ever do that again!' and stormed out of the room."

Is such a response easily forgotten?

"It's been over twenty years since that happened, and I can still see and *feel* vividly what happened."

One vital truth we've learned and seen repeated in our lives and the lives of others is this: *Remaining tender during a trial is one of the most powerful ways to build an intimate relationship* (James 1:19-20).

Most people's usual pattern during times of crisis or high anxiety is to lash out or lecture—or both—especially if the problem is caused by somebody else's mistake. But tenderness and consistent physical reassurance transforms and energizes those around us.

### THE ULTIMATE EXAMPLE

Earlier we spoke of the way God modeled these principles when Jesus walked the back trails and highways of planet Earth. No longer could God be thought of as some distant, unconcerned deity in a far corner of infinity. He came, robed in warm, human flesh. And while He walked among us, He reached out His hands.

The apostle John reflected on that crucial fact when he began his letter to the infant church.

That which was from the beginning, which we have heard, which we have seen with our eyes, which we have looked at *and our hands have touched*—this we proclaim concerning the Word of life (1 John 1:1, emphasis mine).

Jesus seemed to go out of His way to express physical tenderness and reassurance. Once when some dads and moms crowded to the front of the line with their little ones, Christ's self-appointed guard dogs tried to intimidate them and keep them at a respectful distance. Nevertheless,

When Jesus saw this, he was indignant. He said to them, "Let the little children come to me, and do not hinder them, for the kingdom of God belongs to such as these." ...And he took the children in his arms, put his hands on them and blessed them (Mark 10:14,16).

His tenderness in dealing with others emerged in a startling way when a feared and despised leper came to Him. Scripture tells us that "Jesus reached out his hand and touched the man" (Matthew 8:3).

Can't you imagine the people around Jesus flinching from that action? This man was unclean! Dangerous! Communicable! Yet Jesus, in His wisdom, knew the man's need for both spiritual cleansing *and* physical tenderness.

A short time before Jesus went to the cross, Peter, James, and John accompanied Him on a trek to the peak of a high mountain. While they were there, He "was transfigured before them. His face shone like the sun, and his clothes became as white as the light. Just then there appeared before them Moses and Elijah, talking with Jesus" (Matthew 17:2-3).

As if that weren't enough to blow their circuit breakers, a bright cloud came over them and the voice of God the Father spoke. It was too much. The disciples "fell facedown to the ground, terrified." Then, while they were still hugging the turf and shaking in their sandals, they felt a familiar grip on their shoulders. "Jesus came and touched them. 'Get up,' he said. 'Don't be afraid' " (vv. 6-7).

There was that touch...that touch like no other. The touch of a dear Friend. The touch of God.

After the shock and horror of the crucifixion, the grief-wracked disciples needed His touch more than ever. When He suddenly appeared to them behind closed doors, however, they panicked. Could they touch a ghost? Would their hands pass right through Him? He was quick to comfort them. "Why are you troubled, and why do doubts rise in your minds? Look at my hands and my feet. It is I myself! Touch me and see; a ghost does not have flesh and bones, as you see I have" (Luke 24:38-39).

After He ascended into heaven, His followers finally began to understand His intentions. The touch of God had not been removed from among them. While they would not feel the physical warmth of Christ's own hand again until they were reunited in heaven, the Lord had made it clear that *they* were to be His hands and feet on earth. When they touched someone in His love and in His name, *He* was touching that someone.

It's still true today. That frightened young soldier in our opening story felt strong arms around him that night, *and they were the arms of Christ.* It was the Lord Jesus who drew him out of trauma and grief and nightmare into the warmth of God's eternal love. That Young Life leader allowed himself to become the very arms and hands of God.

So must we.

Note

1. Gary Smalley and Dr. John Trent, *The Gift of the Blessing* (Nashville: Thomas Nelson Publishers, 1993).

*Chapter Four*

# BUILDING CHARACTER AND RESPONSIBILITY

I t was supposed to be one of "America's Funniest Home Videos."

The popular television series was screening its best of the best. These were supposed to be the most uproarious homemade mini-productions of the year, candid Americana at its comical peak.

But when they rolled the second place finisher—the one that just missed the $10,000 prize—I (John) had a hard time laughing. It's not that the scene wasn't funny.

It showed a three-year-old girl sitting alone at the table in the family dining room. Her mom and dad had left the room, but she had been directed to stay until she finished her peas. A hidden camera recorded her actions. What she did next was no great surprise. Instead of eating the modest helping of veggies, she rapidly began *hiding* them. Pretty clever, huh? Peas began to magically disappear under cup, plate, place mat, and napkin. (They flatten out so nicely.)

The deed done, her parents came back in to check on her "progress."

"Well, honey, did you eat all your vegetables?"

49

"I sure did, Mom and Dad," the little voice pipes as she holds up a clean plate. "See?"

Big joke. Mom and Dad laugh hilariously. The TV host cracks up. The studio audience goes crazy. Everyone votes for the "little liar" and smiles at how cute she looks. And one little girl's sense of honesty (along with ten million other little girls watching the program across America) takes a direct hit below the waterline from an Exocet missile.

It's not that I can't see the humor in a mini-Watergate cover-up at the dinner table by a three-year-old. When I was four, I was told to wash out the turtle bowl. Rather than doing it the "plain old way," I decided to give my little green friends a bubble bath—right in their bowl. The turtles didn't survive the experience, of course, but even when I was confronted with their clean, bubbly corpses, I tried to deny it. (If they didn't *see* me do it, I must not be guilty, I reasoned at the time.)

Hiding peas under plates and dousing turtles in Mr. Bubble do have a funny side…but such incidents may also point a person down a road that is anything but funny. The Scriptures tell us that lying isn't cute, even if it's captured in a cute setting. As we've seen time and again, to get away with a lie only increases the likelihood of lying again.

This mom and dad might not be laughing too hard as the years go by if they let her "cute" behavior go unchecked. What they will find is that if you teach your child to be dishonest, you can forget all about teaching her *responsibility*.

Why? Because character and responsibility are Siamese twins; they share vital internal organs. You cannot surgically separate them without doing serious damage to both.

When parents ask us how to teach responsibility to their children, many seem to be looking for a *technique*. Something they can jot down on a three-by-five card. A snappy short-cut formula they can carry out of the office in their hip pocket. SEVENTEEN TIMELESS TECHNIQUES FOR TEACHING TOTAL RESPONSIBILITY. (Now, there's a book title for you.) "Isn't there some kind of cassette tape we can play while they're sleeping—maybe slip it in there subliminally?"

Well, yes. There probably is a book, tape, or seminar somewhere like that. But it's interesting…when you open the Scriptures, you read very little about "techniques" in child rearing. What you do read a lot about is *character:* your need of it; your children's need of it; your responsibility to see it develop both in yourself and your family. When it comes to culti-vating character and responsibility, short-cuts are in short supply.

## RESPONSIBILITY COMES THROUGH CHARACTER

We tell parents that if they really want to instill responsibility in a child, they need to concentrate on two specific character traits. If with God's help they can plant these two seedling traits in the lives of their children and nurture them in two fertile soils we will speak of later, responsibility will develop as a matter of course. These two crucial traits are *honesty* and *serving*. The two essential soils necessary for these traits to grow are *fairness* and *consistency*.

### The Seedling of Honesty

Hiding peas under the plate may seem cute now, but the later mani-festations of lying and deception are anything but. Make sure you both *walk and talk* honesty from the earliest days of family life.

I (Gary) remember talking to my little ones about telling the truth. Norma and I used to say, "Do you know what telling one lie makes you?"

"No, what?"

"It makes you a *liar*. Do you know how long it takes to gain back the trust from someone you've lied to?"

"No."

"It takes months…maybe even years."

I told them the story about Jesus and the man possessed by a legion of demons recounted in Mark 5. It's a real cliff-hanger just as it reads in the text, but I acted it out that night to get the point across. Jesus and the disciples had just beached their boat when a wild, hairy man came leap-ing out of the graveyard, running straight for them. He was naked, bleed-ing from a hundred cuts, and screaming at the top of his lungs. You can well imagine that everybody was ready to jump back in the boat, they were so afraid. Everyone but Jesus, that is. He recognized the man's problem and commanded the demons to leave him. The evil spirits obeyed and dashed into a herd of pigs who promptly hurled themselves—squealing and grunting—over a cliff and into the ocean. (The dramatic possibilities in this story are endless.)

I said, "Boy, I tell you what! None of us want demons inside of *us*, do we?"

"Noooo. Huh-uh. No way."

Then I said, "Did you know there is something that can happen with you where you *invite* demons in your life?"

Their eyes widened, and I talked to them about anger and guilt, how it shuts down the light in our life and pushes us into darkness. And when we're filled with darkness we're open to all kinds of terrible temptations. Demons can actually gain a foothold in our heart.

Kari suddenly blurted out, "Dad! I've stolen some things at Smitty's! Gum."

Greg said, "I have too, Dad!"

"Well, kids," I said, "I have a ladder out in the garage that isn't mine. I borrowed it and never took it back. It belongs to the place where I work. Man, we'd better make these things right, because we want to make sure we don't have a guilty conscience."

The kids said, "Yeah! Let's do it!"

The next day we went to see the manager of Smitty's and Greg and Kari confessed taking gum from the store. Then I took them with me to return the ladder. While the kids listened, I had to explain where it had been for the last ten months. The experience made an impression on all of us; the kids have never forgotten it.

Several years ago my youngest son, Michael, had to wrestle with the same issue. One day he called his football coach and reported an injured ankle so he could get out of practice. It later came out that he had lied.

I confronted him on it. "Well, Mike?"

"Dad, I should have gone to practice, I really feel bad about it."

"Okay, but what are you going to do about it?"

"Do? Well...nothin'."

"What do you mean, nothing? Are you going to go back and confess this—admit this? Do you want to keep lying? Do you want to have this problem? Let me tell you, if you go up and confess something to someone, your chances of doing it again are slim to none. It's so embarrassing! So do you want to do the best thing for yourself, or just slide over this thing?"

"Oh, gee, Dad."

I flashed back to a scene from years before. I was sitting in the office of my seminary professor, confessing that I had cheated on reading assignments all semester. I had reported reading more pages than I actually had read. My professor cried and I cried. He didn't change my grade but the pain and humiliation of confessing that deception changed *me*.

Mike, too, went back and confessed, as hard as it was. But I could see a difference in his life after that incident. It changed his attitude about being "sloppy" with the truth. He took another big step toward responsibility.

*The Seedling of Service*

Serving is the other key link in the character chain. If kids can't learn to serve others, they will never learn to be responsible.

At the Trent household, we've tried to make a start on this with our young daughters, Kari and Laura. If a new family moves into our neighborhood, we have the girls bake cookies to take to the new neighbors. If children get the sense that serving is really important—and that's modeled by mom and dad—then that helps them be responsible.

I (John) know a wealthy couple in Dallas who have really struggled with teaching their children servanthood. For one thing, the kids have had almost whatever they've wanted for years. They've become so accustomed to others meeting *their* needs that the idea of "serving" sounded like something from the Middle Ages...or Mars.

The father in that family realized he was getting a late start, but hey, it was better than no start at all! A week or so before the holidays, he said to his family, "We're going to do something different this Thanksgiving."

His teenagers sat up and listened. Usually when he said things like that it meant something exotic. Like para-sailing in the Bahamas.

But not this time. "We're going to go down to the mission," he told them, "and we're going to serve Thanksgiving dinner to some poor and homeless people."

"We're going to *what?*"

"Come on, Dad, you're kidding…aren't you? Tell us you're kidding."

He wasn't. They went along with it because of his firm insistence, but no one was happy about it. For some reason their dad had "gotten weird" and apparently it was something he just had to get out of his system. Serving at the mission! What if their friends heard about it?

No one could have predicted what happened that day. And no one in the family could remember when they had a better time together. They hustled around in the kitchen, dished up turkey and dressing, sliced pumpkin pie, and refilled countless coffee cups. They clowned around with the little kids and listened to old folks tell stories of Thanksgivings long ago and far away.

The dad in the family was thoroughly pleased (would you believe *stunned?*) by the way his kids responded. But nothing could have prepared him for their request a few weeks later.

"Dad…we want to go back to the mission and serve Christmas dinner!"

And they did. As the kids hoped, they met some of the same people they'd become acquainted with at Thanksgiving. One needy family in particular had been on their minds, and they all lit up when they saw them back in the chow line again. Since that time, the families have had several contacts. The pampered teenagers have rolled up their sleeves more than once to serve the family from one of Dallas's poorer neighborhoods.

There was a marked but subtle change in that home. The kids didn't seem to be taking things so much for granted anymore. Their parents found them more serious…more responsible. Yes, it was a late start. But it was a start.

## The Soil of Fairness

For all your good intentions, you won't be able to teach these two vital character traits if your children sense a climate of unfairness in your home.

Let's say that mom and dad are trying to establish some basic groundrules in the "neatness" department. Before the kids leave for school in the morning, the new dictum goes, they need to make their beds and pick up their clothes. That sounds reasonable enough...until they happen to pass the folks' room on the way to breakfast and notice that *their* bed looks like Hurricane Hilda just passed through. By the time they've tripped over dad's Reeboks in the hall and removed mom's gloves from the top of the toaster, they could start getting a little cynical.

Obviously, that's an unfair situation. If the parents want their kids to learn basic disciplines, then they had better ante up with some disciplines of their own.

It's astonishing how early in life children start promoting this concept of "fairness." It seems to be part of the factory-installed equipment that comes in the delivery room. I (John) was reminded of that a couple of years ago when Cindy and I started enforcing some disciplines on TV watching with our daughter, Kari. She would be allowed to watch certain programs at certain times. Then, when the program was over, the TV went off.

I never thought of that little rule as I stretched out one afternoon to watch a pro football double-header. (Do you realize how *long* two football games in a row can seem to a restless three-year-old who wants to play with Daddy?) Just before halftime in the second game, Kari sat down beside me and asked, "Dad, how come you limit *my* TV time and *you* can watch all the football you want?"

Then I realized what I was doing. I was trying to teach her responsibility in TV viewing habits, but was showing none myself. It wasn't fair. That unfairness was like heavy static in my teaching frequency; it made it hard for her to receive my message.

One of the fastest ways to violate that inborn "fairness" principle is by treating one child differently from his siblings. We heard of one man in his forties who for years couldn't speak a civil word to his younger sister. You had to look back to their family history to find out why. His dad had returned from the Korean War when the boy was a toddler. Filled with anger and tension over his war experiences, the father was extremely strict with his son, disciplining him harshly. As the war tensions gradually melted away, he became less severe and demanding. The second child, a daughter, had a much easier go of it. The father had learned some things about patience and tenderness. The oldest boy, however, was deeply embittered by this change. The dad seemed to be showing preference to the younger sibling. The hurt and bitterness eventually settled into a deep enmity toward his sister.

Sound familiar? It's a pattern as ancient as Isaac with his sons Jacob and Esau...and Jacob with *his* sons. If you try to plant character seedlings in the acidic soil of unfairness, there is little chance they will take root.

## The Soil of Consistency

It won't work to give your kids a "weekend seminar" on traits such as honesty and serving and then check out for the rest of the year. Character must be deep-rooted to survive; it reaches way down into the soil of consistent living. It isn't a short term change of behavior that makes an impression on our kids; *it's a life.*

A couple I (John) know have been working hard at planting character seeds in the life of their eleven-year-old foster child. The boy's mother and father are both on death row in the state prison. He pulled the trigger; she drove the getaway car. My friend is providing this boy's *tenth* foster home. His life has been a bewildering journey through a kaleidoscope of changing standards. One home strict and severe. The next open and free. One set of foster-parents who are formal and guarded. The next informal and loosey-goosey.

With God's strength and wisdom—and presuming our friends have adequate time with the boy—they may yet help him to order his tragically scrambled life. But they will need a firm and patient tenderness to plant the boy's torn and damaged roots in the soil of consistent love and discipline.

While most kids will never have to endure such a round-robin of parents and homes, many will still face the insecurity and confusion of parental inconsistency. To the degree that they do, their sense of responsibility will be stunted.

One of my (John's) friends grew up in a tightly-disciplined German home. His best childhood friend was Italian through and through. Once when he was eleven or twelve, he spent the night at this friend's house. The first thing that surprised him was the noise level in that home. Everyone seemed to be talking at once at one volume setting. Loud.

On this night, however, something particularly disturbing seemed to be going on. The boys, supposedly sleeping upstairs in a bedroom, heard loud cries and shouts. They went out on the landing that overlooked the great room below to listen in on the commotion.

Apparently one of the Italian boy's older sisters was very late in getting home from a date. As more time went by, the parents seemed beside themselves with worry, grief, and anger. Even old Grandmother got into the act, yelling as loud as any of them.

"She's been killed! Murdered! Something terrible has happened!"

"Wait'll I get my hands on her—if she's alive!"

Finally she came in the door and everyone came unglued. Weeping. Screaming. Gesturing wildly. How could she treat them this way? Didn't she have any heart at all? Any sense of decency? She deserved to be grounded for fifteen years! They were going to deal with her in the morning!

The boys watched all this from upstairs: the German boy opened-mouthed and pale; his Italian friend smirking and relaxed.

"Gosh," said the overnight guest. "Your poor sister. She's gonna get killed. She's never going to go anywhere again. I just feel so bad for her!"

"Aw," said his friend with a light gesture of dismissal, "they'll forget all about it by morning. It's no big deal."

The German boy was stunned. "Are you kidding? They won't forget that! She's in terrible trouble." In his home, that sister would have been in mortal danger. If his mom and dad said they were going to do something, *they did it!*

"You'll see," his friend smiled, and they headed back to bed.

The next morning at the breakfast table the German boy held his breath as the errant sister stepped lightly down the stairs. *Oh boy*, he thought, *hear it comes!*

Grandmother lit up like sunlight on a window pane. She threw her arms around the girl and gave her a big hug and kiss. "Good morning, good morning, dear. So good to see you!" Everyone else got the same treatment as they came to the table. They were all hugging and kissing each other like they'd been separated for weeks. The German boy's own uncle hadn't received such a welcome when he had been away two years fighting in World War II. He'd walked in the door, accepted a few handshakes and slaps on the back, a polite nod or two, and went straight to his room. It was as though he'd been away for ten minutes.

Our friend's point in telling the story was this: 99 percent of the time moms and dads need to be *Italian* in their warmth, affirming, caring, and physical affection. Then, in the remaining 1 percent of time when they're exercising discipline, they need to be *German*. The best homes are bilingual: they speak Italian and German.[1]

The key word in each instance, however, is consistency!

If kids can see clearly whether we're living a life of character and integrity, our spouse can be directly motivated, or discouraged because of it. That's clearly seen in God's blueprint for courtship and marriage, The Song of Solomon. In the first chapter of this Old Testament book, the first verses speak about the effect character has on Solomon's bride.

"May he kiss me with the kisses of his mouth," she says. While they exhibit great physical restraint until their wedding night (recorded in chapter 4), her passion level is unquestionably present. But why? What's the secret behind her desiring to kiss him repeatedly? The Scriptures tell us,

*"Because your name is like purified oil..."*

In the Old Testament, someone's name stood for who they were, and who they could become. That's why God would change Abram's name to Abraham; and later Simon's to Peter. A person's name stood for who they were, and in this case, Solomon's bride is excited about kissing him because his "name" is a "purified" one.

In Bible times, they purified olive oil by pouring the unrefined oil through trays of various sized rocks. First the oil was poured on trays of larger rocks and the oil would drip through to another tray filled with smaller rocks, then even smaller, until a layer of gravel lay at the bottom.

The pure oil that collected in the cistern beneath these trays of rocks was a picture of her view of his life—refined, honest, free from impurity.

One of the best ways we can leave the light on for our children is to make sure they see our *consistent* love for our spouse. Without a doubt, a purified life is one of the most desirable, motivating aspects of any person's character.

It may even get you a kiss!

Note
1. Robert Barnes, *Who's In Charge Here?* (Dallas: Word Books, 1991).

Chapter Five

# "ARE YOU LISTENING TO ME?"

Whenever we teach on the subject of family communication, I (John) sometimes flash back to a scene from my high school years in our single-parent home. I remember what my twin brother and I used to do when we got back from our double dates.

No matter what time we got in, whether it was 11:30 on a regular weekend, or 2:00 A.M. on prom nights, we would always go into Mom's room, flop down on either side of her on the bed, wake her up, and tell her about the evening.

Sometimes we'd lie there in the dark, talking for hours. It was like stereo for poor Mom, one twin on each side: laughing, remembering, cutting up, dreaming out loud, talking about our plans, hopes, fears, and experiences.

While I'm sure a more sensitive person would have thought of it earlier, at some point it finally dawned on us that Mom had to get up the next morning and go to work to support the family. Maybe she would

61

prefer that we not wake her up and talk her head off on those late nights. I suggested that to her once, and I'll never forget her reply.

"John," she said, "I can always go back to sleep. But I won't always be able to talk to my boys like this."

My mother knew that with two active teenagers, she had to be available to talk when *they* were ready—not just when it was convenient. We always knew we were welcome to talk to her. We always knew our thoughts and experiences were important to her. We always knew we were valued.

Did she have *time* to listen to us? Not really. She worked hard, carried around a heavy load of responsibility, and as a rheumatoid arthritic, would certainly have benefited from some extra sleep. The fact is, she *made time* to listen. By so doing, she said "I love you" in a way two teenaged boys have cherished through the years. Mom knew how to leave the lights on.

When you think about it, what can one human being do for another human being that shows more respect or honor or value than to really listen to that individual? It's a fact: love makes time to listen.

In our counseling, we have witnessed the sickening spectacle of families suddenly beginning to self-destruct. The closeness between mom and dad evaporates like water on a blistering hot Phoenix sidewalk. The kids are unresponsive and begin to drift away. All of this could have been anticipated; they had not spent adequate daily time in meaningful communication. They had never learned to listen to each other.

It's fascinating to consider the way the human body functions— and how much it can teach us about relationships. Just consider the circulatory system.

Each day our heart pumps over 1,800 gallons of blood through 62,000 miles of blood vessels. This constant flow of blood distributes life-giving nutrients throughout the body. As long as this flow remains unobstructed, the body will stay healthy and continue to grow. Yet even a minor constriction of the circulatory system can create major health problems. If we ignore these problems and allow them to continue, our very life can be threatened.

Communication within your family is a great deal like the circulatory system. In a healthy family, communication flows unobstructed. Whether we're merely chatting or sharing the deepest of dreams, family members make a priority of listening to one another. But just as a junk food diet can clog our circulatory system, faulty communication patterns can imperil a family. When we stop listening to each other, it's as though our family suffers a stroke. We become disabled. Certain members no longer respond to other members.

It doesn't have to be that way! Practicing a few helpful listening skills can dramatically change the atmosphere in your home. The needle on the family barometer can move from "Cold and Threatening" to "Warm and Sunny" faster than you might believe possible.

Consider the following ideas carefully.

### LISTEN WITH YOUR WHOLE BODY

It might surprise you to learn that you listen more with your eyes than you do with your ears. Communication experts tell us that words comprise only about 7 percent of communication! Body language is 55 percent and tone of voice 38 percent. So a huge portion of listening is with your eyes.

Think about it. Have you ever tried to talk to someone while his eyes roved around the room? He's saying, "Yeah" and "Um-hmm" and nodding his head, but his attention is not on you. You want to take him by the shoulders and say, "Would you stop looking around and LISTEN to me?!"

Many of us at some time or another have carried on an entire "conversation" with one of our kids while we were absorbed in a television program or reading a magazine. "Uh, huh," and "That sounds good, Honey," uttered with our eyes focused elsewhere does not communicate acceptance to our children.

Solomon the wise dropped an incredibly helpful communication hint when he penned Proverbs 15:30: *"Bright eyes gladden the heart"* (NASB).

Most of us have had the experience of walking into a room and seeing somebody's eyes "light up" when he or she sees us.

That momentary sparkle in another person's eyes communicates volumes. Next time you're at the airport, watch the faces of the people getting off the plane and coming through the gate. Every now and then a man, woman, or child searching the crowd will "make contact" with a loved one in the waiting area. Their eyes suddenly come alive. It's like someone flipping on a light switch. That look says more than words can express. *"I love you. I've missed you. You're important. You mean so much to me. I'm so excited to see you."*

What does your family read about themselves...in your eyes?

What do they "hear" in your body language?

Do your eyes "light up" when you listen? Your family will notice if they do—or don't.

Do you face the person who's talking to you? It sounds so simple, yet so many of us neglect even this basic. Do you put your finger on the place where you were reading when someone in your family wants to say something to you—as if you can't wait for the "interruption" to go away and leave you alone? (Don't worry, it will.)

Real listening means taking some radical steps. Like putting the newspaper down. Or turning off the tube (horrors!). It means leaning forward a little. If the speaker is little, it may mean getting down on your knees. Just imagine yourself five-foot-five living in a world populated by nine-foot giants. It gets tiresome craning your neck all the time!

Real listening means letting your eyes light up. Raising your eyebrows. Expressing your interest verbally once in awhile. "Oh, WOW! Unbelievable! Is that right? Are you kidding? How about that." Kids will tend to keep talking about a subject if they see someone is actually listening to them! They will also feel honored, valued, and warmed down to their toes.

The opposite is also true. If you lean back, look away, or appear distracted and disinterested, you shut down the conversation. You turn out the lights in their eyes. Although members of your family may never have taken a class in "body English," they can "read" all too clearly when you are no longer interested in them.

## ACTIVITY CAN BE A GATEWAY TO MEANINGFUL COMMUNICATION

We spoke earlier about the importance of shared experiences in family bonding. Those activities also can provide invaluable opportunities to listen to one another.

People in Bible times seem to have enjoyed a lot more opportunity for this kind of interaction. Moses urged the moms and dads of Israel to talk about love for God and the importance of His commands in the course of everyday affairs. "Impress [these commands] on your children," he wrote. "Talk about them when you sit at home and when you walk along the road, when you lie down and when you get up" (Deuteronomy 6:7).

How often does a modern family "walk along the road" together, enjoying the quiet, pointing out object lessons in the world of nature around them? Those sorts of conversations occurred more naturally in the flow of daily life a few generations ago. Today, we have to work harder to provide such opportunities. Simply being together on family outings and adventures allows time for talk to develop that would probably never occur in the car on the way to ballet lessons or soccer practice.

Again, it's not the activity itself that's so important, it's the meaningful conversations that develop both coming and going.

In ten years as a youth pastor, I (Gary) learned that I probably wasn't going to have much interaction with my kids during the canoe trip or the camping experience itself. I knew that my real ministry would come on the bus! Or on the walk. Or sitting down with someone at a meal. I knew that ahead of time, so I looked and waited for any opportunity. When our family went on camping trips in our mini motor home, I knew great dialogue wouldn't flow while we threw fish lines in the water or conquered a steep hiking trail. The really profound conversations would take place late at night, when one of the kids would crawl into the front seat with me while I drove to "keep Daddy awake."

My wife, Norma, was really good at drawing the kids out during their growing up years. She always seemed to be on the lookout for opportunities to ask questions and probe their thoughts.

What a wonderful heritage…a mom or dad who really listens! If you had that kind of parent, you have no idea how blessed you are. So many have deeply longed for that listening parental ear—and not finding it, have carried the pain for the rest of their lives.

You can be that listening parent! What a wonderful way to light up your home—and kindle unquenchable memories!

### ARGUMENTS CAN BE DEFUSED THROUGH "QUICK LISTENING"

*Quick listening* is one method you can use to help you understand what another family member is really saying. It slows conversation to a manageable pace, allowing understanding to overtake and pass out-of-control emotions.

It's a helpful tool to use when an argument is about to boil over, and it is also very useful in everyday conversation to improve our understanding of one another. Here are three simple steps to help you get the picture.

*1. Try to "see through" to the issue behind the issue.*

Let's pretend you and I are having a discussion and it's beginning to spill over into a disagreement. We're having difficulty understanding each other and your body language tells me you just might be getting upset. (Maybe it's that grip you have on the front of my shirt!) Using quick listening, I can honor you by giving you the opportunity to clarify what you're saying without a response from me. It lets you know that I'm genuinely concerned and interested in what you're saying—and that I'm making an effort to understand you. It relaxes you because you realize I'm more interested in comprehending what you say than merely winning an argument. It also allows me another opportunity to hear what you're trying to say.

*2. Restate what the other person has said in your own words.*

After you have had the opportunity to summarize what you've said to me, I can respond, "Now let me repeat what you've said to make sure I understand." I can then verbalize what you've said to see if I've actually received the message *you* meant to communicate.

If I have it right, you might say, "Yes, that's it." If not, you will say, "No." Then I can restate what you've said. It's my responsibility at that point to keep asking questions and rewording your statement until I get a "yes." When I do, it's my turn to tell you how I feel. That way we're both honored in what is said.

### 3. Lovingly limit your own words.

Using too many words during an important discussion can actually break down intimate conversation. If I were to ramble on and on, I would increase the chances that you the listener will react to what I say without understanding my points. If I continue to pile up my words without clarifying the issues and feelings we have, you might become so frustrated or bored that you'll tune me out altogether.

Once again, Solomon was on target when he wrote: "When there are many words, transgression is unavoidable, but he who restrains his lips is wise" (Proverbs 10:19, NASB).

Quick listening has stopped numerous arguments from igniting around the Smalley and Trent households, and we know it can make a difference in your family as well. One of the keys to any healthy relationship is a willingness to say, "I'm more interested in understanding what you're saying than in thinking of what I'm going to say once you're done talking."

## THOUGHTFUL QUESTIONS CAN OPEN UP THE DOOR

Meaningful communication is sharing your feelings, goals, and ideas—your very personhood. But it isn't always easy to express those deeper things with one another. That's why it helps to have a few thoughtful questions on hand to throw out at one of those special moments when you sense openness in your child.

I (Gary) loved to set up imaginary scenarios for my kids. I would say things like, "Let's pretend you are thirty-five years old. Tell me who you're married to, how many kids you have, where you live, and what you're

LEAVING THE LIGHT ON

doing." When the kids would see that I was seriously interested—not just kidding around—they would begin to open up and tell me things I never knew about them. I started this when they were in junior high.

There's another question I love to ask my family. I say: "Okay, it's January—or July, or whatever. One year from now, what would you love to see happen in your life so that if it happens, you would say, 'Wow! What a *great* year!' What would it take to make the next twelve months a '10' on a scale of one to ten?" After thinking about it, they start saying things like, "Boy, if this or that happened this would be a great year!" That one question opens up incredible insights into their dreams and desires and goals. And it's all spontaneous, because it's what *they* want, not what I "want to hear."

## SIMPLE WORD PICTURES OPEN DOORS, TOO

When the children are very young, questions may not be enough to enhance understanding. I (John) observed how this worked with our daughter, Kari. When she was two-and-a-half to three years old, she was going through a tantrum stage. When Cindy or I would say, "Kari, it's time to pick up your toys," she would cry and fall down on the floor and roll around. Obviously, this behavior warranted discipline at times, but we really wanted to help her understand the problem and even to help her begin to learn the discipline of self-control.

So after one such weeping and wailing episode, Cindy and I took a clear glass full of water and put it in the microwave. We had Kari push the buttons to about four minutes—allowing the water to boil over. As it started to bubble and boil and spill, we let her push the "pause" button and watch as the water became calm again. Then we talked to her about it.

"Kari, you know, that's kind of what *you* do sometimes. You're like the glass of water." (Her eyes got very big. We had her attention.) "When you get all upset it's like you're bubbling up inside, but when you push the pause button the bubbles go away, don't they? Mommy and Daddy have had to learn how to push the pause button and you can learn how, too!"

We've used many such word pictures with her to get our point across and to help her understand her own emotions—and they've worked better than we've ever dreamed.

With small children, you have to find a way to make the intangible tangible. When they are having trouble expressing themselves, you may want to set an object down in front of them. Let's say it's a book. "If you were a book," you might ask, "what kind of book would you be? Out of all the little books that you have, which one would describe what you're going through today—which story?" If they can't say anything, you just keep asking questions. "Is it the one about Winnie the Pooh getting stuck in the hole?" If they say, yes, you probe a little deeper and find out more.

Still not convinced that kids are sophisticated enough to be affected by word pictures or use them?

This summer I (John) was speaking at a family camp. One afternoon my two daughters, Kari and Laura, donned life preservers and we all went out for a canoe ride.

Little Laura was barely three, and this was her very first voyage in a canoe. From her place seated at the bottom of the canoe, she could hardly see over the gunnels. And while I enjoy canoeing and am fairly adept at it, there were times when we became a little "tipsy" in the water. After one scary wobble out over deep water, Laura looked back at me, her eyes round as saucers.

"Daddy!" she blurted out. "My stomach has a headache!"

Children of all ages love stories—and word pictures. So don't underestimate their power, even in the life of a little one.

Yes, some of the communication helps in this chapter take time and thought and discipline to develop and employ. It takes perseverance—and the very strength and courage of God's Spirit—to replace impatience, insensitivity, and self-preoccupation, with loving communication patterns. No, working on family communication isn't easy.

But then again, neither is the alternative.

# VALUING OUR DIFFERENCES

**M**y wife and I are so different, one of the few things we had in common was that we were both married on the same day! When I (John) was courting Cindy, these differences gave us a lot of laughs.

She thinks stoplights are put into the world to bring order to life. I think they're a tool to disrupt our lives. She likes to balance the checkbook to the penny; I like to switch banks so that I finally know what my balance is. I'm a spender, she's a saver. I get energy from being with people—lots of people. Cindy gets energy from being with only a few people—or just one. I'm right handed; she's left-handed. The list goes on and on.

When we were courting, we told ourselves, "We're going to be a great team. What a strength!" Yet within a year, the same characteristics that had attracted us to each other were the very things that most irritated us.

We're not alone. In couple after couple we talk with across the country, people find that what was so cute in courtship, can become killing in the

71

confines of marriage. Survey after survey shows that the number one reason for mate selection is the *differences* between individuals. Like two halves of the apple, we meet at church or a party and finally feel like a complete, whole, Washington State Golden Delicious apple. Yet in less than a year of marriage, many of these same relationships will be applesauce.

In a recent study of couples married more than twenty-five years, one finding was consistent. Those couples who rated their relationship as close and mutually satisfying had something important in common—they all knew how to value their spouse's differences.

In short, differences can become a devastating source of conflict in a marriage and family. Time and again we've seen those marital differences "shoot out the lights" of a home. And yet learning the skills of recognizing and valuing each other's differences can be one of the most positive things you do.

Let's face it, learning to recognize and value our differences is a necessity, not a luxury. As our good friends Chuck and Barb Snyder are fond of saying, "Men and women are so different that marriage in itself is grounds for incompatibility!"

When a "very different" husband marries a "very different" wife and they become the parents of "very different" children, it becomes even *more* crucial to understand and appreciate one another's natural strengths. Despite our differences, we *can* learn to build family teamwork and harmony.

## IF IT'S A BENT, DON'T FIX IT

A familiar verse in Scripture may have more counsel on this subject than many of us have realized. Proverbs 22:6 tells us to "train a child in the way he should go, and when he is old he will not turn from it." A good translation of that verse in the original language would be "train up a child according to his way" or "*according to his bent.*"

All of us seem to come uniquely wired with a bent. One particular child (a combination of the first and last bent we'll discuss) may be by far the most difficult to discipline. Another may easily be the most sensitive and prone to be hurt by your words. Parents who ignore these fundamental differences can unknowingly inflict unbelievable discouragement and pressure on their children.

Let's take a brief look at the four basic bents resident in most families. Then, in a following chapter, we'll consider how these differences can actually be blended together into a close-knit home. But just before we start our look at the family zoo, it's important to realize two things: First, we're all a combination of these four basic bents to some extent. We know of no "purebreds." Usually, however, one or two basic bents will predominate in a person's interactions with others. Second, these areas of personality strengths can be *developed.* The idea that our personality traits are set in concrete may sell books, but it doesn't square with the facts. We've seen in our own lives—and in the lives of hundreds across the country—that people can achieve a high degree of balance in their lives.

## MAKE WAY FOR THE LION

Lions are strong, aggressive, take-charge types. If you have a child with a large amount of Lion in him, he is basically letting *you* live at home!

We heard a story recently about a five-year-old Lioness who had just started kindergarten. She came home from her very first day and slammed the front door! Her startled dad looked up from his lunch.

"My goodness," he said. "What's the matter?"

The little lady banged her lunchbox down on the kitchen table and said, "Daddy, I am *not* going back to that school!"

"Really? How come?"

"Because that teacher didn't do one thing I told her to!"

There's a Lion cub for you. They grow up being assertive, get-to-the-bottom-line leaders. They're usually doers, rather than watchers or listeners, and they love to solve problems.

If you're a teacher with Lion kids, they're probably running the class—or *at least trying to.* That attitude tends to carry on in life where they usually end up as the boss at work—or at least they think they are!

Properly balanced, their charge-ahead, take-no-captives mindset can be a tremendous strength. They make fearless Marines, tough managers, and determined, visionary entrepreneurs. Are they decisive? Absolutely. With or without the facts, *let's make a decision!*

Their natural strength at making quick decisions tends to spill over into their conversations. When it comes to meaningful communication, the average Lion wants it like *Reader's Digest*, not *War and Peace*.

As a result, do Lions tend to be great at chit-chat? Usually not. After all, what's the point? An insensitive Lion would be capable of talking to his or her spouse for five or ten minutes, then interrupting and saying, "Honey, this is great, but the next time we talk—try having a point!"

Casual chatter, after all, doesn't have a "purpose." It doesn't *solve* anything. (Let's at least get into an argument! Then we can get all our cards on the table.)

What's the common time frame for a Lion? Usually it's *NOW*. If you have a child who is a Lion, when does he want breakfast? NOW. When does she want to go to the mall? NOW. A Lion boss will slap a project on your desk and say, "I want this done NOW."

"But," you might protest. "You just gave me a project to work on ten minutes ago."

"I know," the Lion will likely reply. "But that was then, this is NOW!"

As you look around the country, you will see Lions in many places of leadership, whether in business or ministry. Without Lions, there would be a lot more discussed and a lot less accomplished in our world. It's a valuable character trait, but it needs to be held in balance.

What are some things Lions need to learn?

First, they need to accept the fact that *questions are not challenges to their authority*. Most Lions do not like to be questioned. They would rather just be obeyed! In particular, they can resent the close questioning of more detailed personality types who ask things like, "Why are you doing that?" or, "Have you really thought through what this decision means to our family?" To a Lion, words like that can often sound like a challenge or criticism. Yet most often, those who love to ask questions do so out of their strength of being detailed and careful, not from being critical.

The second thing Lions need to learn is that *projects are not as important as people.* Lions can get totally wrapped up in the challenge of completing a "task." In the process, they can steamroll people who appear to be "slowing up the process."

Confronted with the prone figure of a flattened co-worker, a Lion will look down and say, "Hey, I wasn't criticizing YOU, I was just criticizing your WORK." Yet not all of us can make that kind of separation. For some temperaments, if you attack their work, you are attacking *them.*

Great strengths reside in those who possess this temperament. Yet they need the strengths of a second basic personality type, those we call Otters.

## OTTERS: PARTIES WAITING TO HAPPEN

Have you ever seen an Otter that wasn't having fun? Watch a "National Geographic" special, and you'll see them sliding down creek beds and floating on their backs, eating food off their stomachs. In the world of human personalities, Otters tend to exhibit similar characteristics. They tend to be energetic, fun-loving souls. Otter kids love to hang around at their friends' houses, or want their friends over…*constantly.* They wake up with the conviction that life could be, ought to be, or will be *fun.* Ever excitable, otters are enthusiastic cheerleaders and motivators. Their favorite habitat is an environment where they can talk (and talk and talk and talk) and have the opportunity to give lots of input on major decisions. For example, many Otters don't get into carpools to save the environment; they so do because it gives them a captive group to talk to!

Otters' outgoing nature makes them consummate networkers. They usually know people who know people who know people. The only problem is, they can't remember anyone's name! Everyone is "Old Buddy" or "Sweetheart," but even though they know a thousand people one inch deep, they communicate so much genuine warmth that they are often everyone's best friends. They can be soft and encouraging with others (unless under pressure, when they tend to use their verbal skills to attack). Because of their strong desire to be liked, however, they can often fail to be hard on problems now—which results in problems compounding down the road.

We bump into lots of Otters at our seminars. For one reason, the Smalley/Trent seminars happen to be taught by a couple of playful Otter-types. But what these people actually come to our seminars for are the *breaks!* Yes! Where else can you drink coffee and circulate with two thousand new people (with nametags!) who are interested in relationships? It's Otter heaven.

Cindy and I (John) have close to a pure-bred Otter in our nearly five-year-old daughter, Kari. She always has a mischievous twinkle in her eye and whenever it gets quiet around the house when she's awake, we both call out, "Kari, what are you doing?" Usually, it's something fun like making a line of Cheerios from the kitchen to her bedroom so she won't get lost, or seeing how many clothes she can put on at the same time and still get them buttoned.

Our family was dining at a Mexican restaurant some time ago, and Kari ordered her usual hot dog. We really do work hard at teaching the children proper manners...but while we were busy eating, Kari was busy dipping her hot dog in her ice water, and then eating it.

It was the waitress who came along and took an exaggerated interest in what she was doing. "You know, honey," she said, "that's an interesting way to eat a hot dog."

"Well, I'm not having a hot dog," Kari replied with a big smile. "I'm having a *cold* dog."

When she saw that got a laugh out of the waitress, she then proceeded to dip the soggy dog into her milk. "Now it's a *milk* dog." Before we were done, she wanted to demonstrate a sugar dog, a Sweet n' Low dog, a salt dog, a coffee dog...anything for a laugh.

Otters are great motivators and encouragers—but how are they at details? Well, not exactly great. An Otter student will typically wait until the night before the due date to get started on his term paper—only to discover that all the reference books have already been checked out of the library. Does he despair? Not an Otter!

He'll simply pick up a box of donuts, find out who's got some books at home, and drop by for a "term paper party."

What's the time perspective of these fun-loving characters? With the Lion it is LET'S DO IT NOW! With the Otter, it's THE FUTURE! That's one reason they're so optimistic all the time.

For an Otter, all of life's problems can either be relegated to the present or the past. If they're in the past, you can't do anything about them. If they're in the present…hey, things are going to work out great tomorrow! That's why one favorite Otter expression is "Lighten up!" They have a tremendous ability to put off worrying until another day.

What do Otters need to learn?

At some point in their romp through life, Otters need to be reminded that their happy-go-lucky antics can create not-so-funny problems…for themselves and others. Even though they dislike bothering with details, they need to get used to the idea that actions have consequences—and not all of them pleasant.

Case in point? *Deadlines are not guidelines.* Sometimes the consequences of failing to complete a job on time cannot be shrugged away. Opportunities can be lost—perhaps irretrievably—and people can be hurt or disappointed when an Otter makes a promise, and then doesn't follow through. Otters can benefit from a strong dose of reality on this score.

In addition, Otters also need to remember that *it is more critical to be a God-pleaser than a people-pleaser.* Parents must be aware that this type of child is highly susceptible to peer pressure. They want so much to be liked and accepted that they may find themselves tempted to "revise" their standards and principles to get along with their friends.

We've looked at a Lion's strength of character, and at how an Otter just tries to be a character. Now, let's look at the type of person who reflects depth of character.

## GOLDEN RETRIEVERS: LOYAL AND TRUE-BLUE

True to their namesake, Golden Retrievers are loyal, supportive, nurturing encouragers. All the Girl Scouts selling cookies within a twenty-mile radius know where these people live, because they have such a difficult time saying no. A Retriever may have already purchased twelve boxes of butterscotch creams, but if he sees a teardrop in a little girl's eye, he'll usually justify buying "just one more box."

To their credit, Retrievers can stoutly absorb a great deal of relational bumps and bruises and yet stay committed. They are listeners and empathizers and make steadfast, be-there-when-ya-need-me friends.

Forget telling "dead cat" jokes to these people, however, because you will not find an appreciative audience. In addition, like a Patriot missile battery, they have an incredible radar detection device that God has built within them to sense "hurting" people. Ever-sensitive and natural counselors, Retrievers can somehow locate the one hurting or depressed person in a roomful of noisy people.

With all their skills at people-helping, however, there is one word Retrievers need to learn—even if it means practicing it in front of the mirror for half an hour each day. It's a small word, but it can make all the difference in their relationships.

You guessed it. It's the word "no."

When pushed to an extreme, each of our great strengths can become liabilities. When for the sake of "loyalty" or "adaptability" a Golden Retriever gives in again and again to the relational demands of another—even when that other person desperately needs a firm "no"—it becomes a situation psychologists call "co-dependency." Retrievers need to learn that genuine love has a hard side as well as a soft side.

A Retriever's time frame is THE PRESENT. They're focused on today's conversations and relationships. Put a Lion personality in a mountain cabin for a month—by himself—and when you return to pick him up, he'll have blown out walls, added on five rooms, and mowed down the trees to put in a mini-mart next door. Otters, alone in a mountain cabin, would somehow sneak in a portable phone, fax, and TV. But if you could ever get a Golden Retriever to leave his family for a month and be by himself, he would adapt splendidly. He'd catch up on his correspondence, make gifts for special friends, and basically blend into his surroundings.

Parents of Golden Retrievers will sometimes be surprised to find *themselves* being parented.

*"You look sad, Mommy, what's wrong?"*

*"Is everything going okay at work, Dad? Are you still worried about your boss being angry at you?"*

Although these concerned children may seem like welcome and convenient sounding boards on some occasions, parents should exercise caution about "opening up" or "dumping" adult burdens on these willing little listeners. We often talk in counseling with a now grown man or woman who is still suffering from carrying too much, too fast. Golden Retriever kids will quietly step under your load with shoulders that weren't meant to carry that sort of emotional weight.

Lions, Otters, and Golden Retrievers. All are tremendous people with valuable strengths. But our list of personalities and personal strengths wouldn't be complete without another important member of the family zoo—our Beaver friends.

## LEAVE IT TO THE BEAVERS

Of all God's creatures, one of the most special are beavers. One story I (John) recently heard from a fishing guide in Alaska points out a major characteristic in these animals—and their human counterparts, as we shall see.

Several hours outside Anchorage, near Mt. McKinley, there was a small road with a round culvert built under it to drain away water. A local beaver looked at that pipe and somehow figured out that if he dammed it up, the water would soon collect into a pool behind it. An instant beaver pond!

Without tape measure or yardstick, he managed to gnaw down a tree and bite off the branches so precisely that the log fit perfectly into the pipe—damming up the water flow. The beaver did such a workman-like job that the road service was unable to remove it from the culvert. The log fit so snugly and securely that the road crew was forced to rip out the road, remove the culvert (log still intact), and re-lay a new pipe. That, friends, is attention to detail!

A human Beaver's unshakable motto is LET'S DO IT RIGHT. If we're not going to do it right, then let's not do it! Combine that natural precision with bulldog persistence and you have an unbelievable employee. Just like the Energizer rabbit on the TV commercials, they keep going and going and going.

Detail-oriented, careful, methodic, and thorough to a fault, these are the type of people who actually read instruction books! In fact, one tremendous strength of a Beaver in the average home is that they're the only ones who can figure out how to set the clock on the VCR!

Do all animals in the family zoo slow down like a Beaver to make sure they're following the directions? Nope. Give an Otter a computer at work, and before he reads anything, he'll have the thing out of the box, plugged in, and be searching the menus for a game to play. Give a Beaver a computer at work and he will want to read the instructions before he takes it out of the box.

It's often easy to spot a Beaver. You know you have a Beaver child if she lines her shoes up in straight lines in her closet. Beavers' blouses or shirts are always color coordinated and hung in a row, and they even roll their socks up! (Otters on the other hand have sock *rooms,* not sock drawers!)

These people are God's architects. They tend to think in columns, square corners, and straight lines. Beavers have a strong need to do things "right" and "by the book." They like maps, charts, and organization. Count on them for quality control functions at home or the office.

Michelangelo, an obvious Beaver, spent seven-and-a-half years *on his back* painting the ceiling of the Sistine chapel. How long would it have taken a Lion to paint that ceiling?

*"We're gonna get a crew in there and we'll knock that sucker out in a week!"*

An Otter never would have finished! After getting a group of his friends to hang out with him on the scaffolding, the work party would soon degenerate into paint fights. (That is, if he remembered to order the paint.)

A Golden Retriever might not finish because she'd constantly be taking all the worker's emotional temperatures.

*"How's it going today? How's the family? You have a stiff neck from laying on your back? Hey, you'd better take the day off and see a chiropractor. Let me work your shift for you."*

If you want something done right, and in a way that will last a lifetime—then leave it to a Beaver. They don't stop on a project until the thing is D-O-N-E. Then, they can look back for the rest of their lives with a deep inward glow, remembering that *they did it right.*

For that reason, a Beaver's time perspective is THE PAST. What counts with them is a consistent track record.

Do you begin to get an idea of how many different "animals" can be under the same roof? Is life a zoo for you sometimes? Does your home feel like "Wild Kingdom"?

There's hope! In the next chapter we'll talk about how these animals can be roped together on the same dog sled and mush in the same direction...and what happens when they don't!

Stay tuned.

# BLENDING OUR DIFFERENCES

O tters live for change.

When John and I (Gary) go to a restaurant, the menu is simply a list of suggestions, a mere starting point where any number of innovations and combinations can begin. Signs like "no substitutions" aren't to be taken seriously. When two Otters are trying to order, the waitress usually earns her tip simply by being patient!

For someone like my wife, Norma, who is *not* an Otter, those sorts of shifts and modifications can be frustrating...and embarrassing. Sometimes as we walk into a restaurant, my Beaver wife will plead with me, "Listen, could you please just take the menu at face value this time?" Frustrated by that restriction, I find myself wanting to redecorate the place. "Hey, do you mind if we move the table over here where the light's better?"

After nearly thirty years of marriage, I continue to marvel at what gets Norma excited. She likes to get up at 5:30 in the morning, head for the office, and plunge into the details for hours at a time...which would have me climbing the walls in no time at all. She loves roots and stability, while I could be content changing homes and neighborhoods every other year. She loves deep relationships, and always wants to contact people we've known in other cities in years past…and that doesn't thrill me at all.

If we hadn't taken the time to really understand and appreciate each other's temperaments, we would find ourselves mocking and degrading each other, which is exactly what we did for years. Now we don't. We've learned to value and admire each other for who we are.

Let's face it. The bents we discussed in the last chapter create enormous differences in the way people think, plan, work, and relax. Parents must continually remember that each of their children may respond to various situations in a completely different way from his siblings…or parents.

### WHEN BENTS BUMP SHOULDERS

Let's say you are a fifth-grade teacher, and one afternoon you give your class an assignment to create a soldier out of clay. Each child receives one pound of clay *and a twenty minute time limit.*

Now take a step back and watch. How do the four different "bents" respond to the challenge? Here's a likely scenario:

You can count on the Lions to finish on time. In fact, they will probably whip something out in five minutes and then spend the remaining time creating boats and tanks and stuff *they* want to make. They know what they want to do. They're in charge!

Your Otters will probably never make it by the time the buzzer rings, but they'll have a great time anyway!

"Hey, look at my guy! Boom! Boom! Gotcha! All right!"

It shouldn't surprise you when they try to organize the task into a group activity. "Look, you make the legs, you make the body, I'll make the arms, and then we'll stick 'em all together and see what it looks like!"

Your Golden Retrievers will probably finish right on time, just because they want to please you so much. But they might *not* finish if they notice one of their little friends struggling.

"Did you get the instructions? Are you doing okay? Don't be discouraged! Are you kidding? That's a terrific rifle—I mean *arm*—I knew it was his arm."

What about your Beavers? Will they finish? *In twenty minutes? Are you kidding?* "You mean we get only *twenty* minutes? That's ALL? How can you make anything *decent* in twenty minutes? I need at least an hour." Despairing of creating an entire soldier, they might concentrate instead on designing an engraved saber or bayonet...or maybe some little buttons for the soldier's coat, with "U.S. Army" or "Special Forces" in tiny printing.

Now let's imagine that these little "animals" have grown up and work together in the same office. 'Tis the season for the office Christmas party. Guess who gets the thing rolling?

"Hey, we're having a Christmas party," the Lion announces. "You WILL be there. I may or may not show up, depending on my work load."

The Otters respond with excitement. "A party! Yeah, let's do it!" The only problem is, they're already attending three other parties that night. No matter, they'll still drop by and talk to *everyone* in the room. After all, it's not a successful party unless you yak with at least forty people. (In fact, you can usually tell when you're talking to an Otter at a party because he's looking past you to the *next* interesting person to talk to!)

Golden Retrievers will show up at the party whether they want to come or not. After all, they would hate to disappoint anybody. And who do *they* talk to at the Christmas party? One person. Probably the same person they drove with. The person they see every morning in the car pool—and if possible, the same person they went to grade school and high school with.

They'll spend the whole time together off to one side, talking deeply and earnestly. Or perhaps they'll spot someone who seems to be depressed. They've picked up on some pain with their long-range relational radar: *nyiing, nyiing, nyinng, BEEP!* They'll find a quiet corner and engage in coffee-cup counseling with this individual for hours.

Beavers are very important to the party. Mostly because they are the only ones who remember to bring food (it was on the list). These are also the folks who will pitch in and clean up after the party so the office will be neat and tidy on Monday morning. (The Otters are long gone by this time, circulating through party #3.)

Now, how in the world do you blend all these bents into some kind of harmony at home?

Let us give you three simple methods that have worked well in each of our family zoos!

*1. Realize that your natural strengths are going to expose a different personality's natural weaknesses.*

If parents don't take time to understand their child's natural bent, they can sometimes cause stress and pressure without even realizing it. It's something that happened to a close friend of ours and his son.

Jim Brawner has a wonderful family and a book on "blending differences" that we highly recommend.[1] His son, Jason, was fast approaching the time when he would get a driver's license. For several years, Jason had been saving for a car, and finally our friend decided to help his son locate a vehicle for transportation to work and school. Here's what happened:

A thorough-going Beaver, Jim reads through all the consumer reports on used cars and goes out "to do it right." Jason, however, is an emotional, excitable Otter. He's absolutely beside himself with anticipation. "I'm getting a car! All right!"

So they go out on a Saturday to spend the afternoon car shopping. Jason is excited about the very first car they encounter through an ad in the paper. It's beautiful, it sounds great, the price is right, and he's ready to grasp those keys in his sweaty palms and *go cruise.* Jim, however, insists on being thorough. He takes a solid hour going over the car in minute detail. He has it analyzed by a mechanic. He lifts up the carpeting, staring at the floorboards like a fortune teller gazing at tea leaves. The longer they crawl over, around, and under this car, the more excited Jason becomes. They test drive it. Jason gets the feel of the wheel. He likes the way it smells. He likes the radio. He likes the way the turn signal goes KA-BINK, KA-BINK, KA-BINK.

After two hours of this, however, Jim decides, no, this isn't the car after all and they climb into the family wagon and drive away to look at the next prospect.

Jason is crushed. Jim is whistling, thoroughly enjoying this detailed search for "the perfect car." They look at four cars that afternoon, and four times Jason rides the emotional roller coaster. Late that evening they return home empty-handed.

Jim is well-pleased, feeling the whole excursion has been educational. The next time out, they'll be that much closer to their goal.

The following Saturday, however, Jim is stunned when his son says, "You go ahead, Dad, I don't want to go."

"You don't want to *go*? How come? This is going to be your car."

"Just go ahead and do it, Dad. Pick out the best one. Then when you're sold on it, come pick me up and I'll look at it."

Jim doesn't understand, so Jason tries a word picture with him. "Dad, you know what you do to our dog? You take a piece of bread, lay it in on Bandit's nose, and say 'STAY!' And poor Bandit sits real still and leaves the bread sitting right there on his nose—even though he's trembling and slobbering all over the place and dying to eat it. He wants that bread so bad, but you've trained him to obey. Then when you say, 'Okay,' Bandit flips up the piece of bread with his muzzle, catches it in his mouth, and eats it with one gulp."

Jim shrugs his shoulders. He isn't getting the connection.

"Well, Dad, I think I feel just like Bandit when you tell him to stay. That's just what you're doing with me. You take me out to look at these neat cars, and it's like you're putting a piece of bread right on my nose. My mouth is watering like crazy and I get all excited, but you never say 'Okay.' "

Jim finally got the picture. Since he loved the challenge of the "hunt," and loved charting out all the details, he assumed Jason would also enjoy the process. The best plan, he now realized, would be to go out alone, critically analyze half a dozen cars, and then narrow it down to one or two he had already "prequalified." Then he and Jason could go out and really enjoy the process together.

I (John) can remember an Otter-Beaver standoff a little closer to home. My wife Cindy is a Beaver and the daughter of a Beaver. I'm close to being a pure-bred Otter. Cindy's dad was a builder, and with what she learned from him, she could probably build a house right now with her own two hands. Beavers are great at putting things together.

But I grew up in a single parent home where we didn't have so much as a hammer. Early in our marriage, Cindy would do things to me that exposed my weakness. Our first home was one of these "buy-a-bargains," and I decided to go through the house and change all the rusty, grimy hardware. To this day I can remember standing in the hallway in the stifling Dallas summer heat, trying to get a new hinge to go on a door. After what seemed like a thousand trials and errors, I was ready to take those hinges back to my friendly Ace hardware guy and stuff them down his throat. (Remember, Otters can attack under pressure.)

Cindy came walking down the hall, took one look at the errant hinge, and casually *turned it over.* It fit perfectly. Then, with a little shrug of her shoulders, she continued down the hall, humming a light little tune. I stared at that hinge and did a slow burn. I was unbelievably angry. Her natural strength had quickly exposed my natural weakness, and it didn't exactly thrill me.

However, I could and often would do the same thing to her. As an Otter, I could step into a roomful of strangers at church and immediately strike up a conversation. Cindy, however, would be more reserved and often end up talking with just one person. Then I would criticize her for not being "friendly" and mingling with others. My natural strength was exposing her natural weakness...and it was dimming the lights in our relationship.

After two years of this tension, it was clear that I wanted her to be an Otter *like me*, and she wanted me to be a Beaver *like her*. It never occurred to me that I might be out of balance. It never occurred to me that I was trying to make her over into my own Otter image—even though it was her steady, sunny, Beaver qualities that had drawn me to her in the first place.

Darryl DelHousaye, our much beloved pastor, has a favorite saying that is tremendously convicting: "The stronger person always initiates the peace." And one day I realized that if there was tension around the house when it came to our blending differences, I needed to be strong. I needed to start valuing my wife for the person she was. Once I made that decision, it was amazing how I began to look differently at her. Before, I resented the way she would ask me to "slow down" and not take every speaking engagement that came along. Today, with two kids who need quantity—not just quality—time, I thank God for my wife's time management skills. Before, I'd be frustrated that she didn't want to buy the couch *now* on credit when it was on sale. Today, I've seen time and again that after waiting to pay cash for something, we'll still find it on sale—plus save all that interest!

With the Lord's help, her outstanding qualities have begun to balance out my out-of-balance Otter qualities—and the Lord certainly knew I needed some balancing out.

*2. Look at the person of Christ as a model of balance.*

When I had first taken the personality test and realized I was an off-the-chart Otter, I felt almost defensive about it. If Cindy would object to the way I was handling something, I would reply, "Hey, you married me. This is the kind of animal I am, so you'll just have to learn to live with it. I'm not going to change."

Although I didn't realize it at the time, saying "That's just the way I am" was the same as saying, "I'm really not serious about becoming like Christ." How is that true?

During His earthly life, Jesus demonstrated a beautiful balance of each of the personality bents. His love was held in balance. He knew when to be hard on problems, and how to be soft with people.

Lions and Beavers tend to be hard on problems. They can be good at that. But they can also be hard on people who don't "measure up." Otters and Retrievers tend to be soft on people. But they can be soft on problems, too—even when love demands a hard side.

89

If our natural strengths tend to push us out-of-balance in our love, the magnet that can pull us back to a life of balance is patterning our life after the person of Christ.

Did Jesus Christ have any Lion in Him? He was called the Lion of Judah (Revelation 5:5). Was He take-charge? The crowds were stunned by the *authority* with which He taught. Even the very wind and waves of the sea bowed to that authority. Was He decisive? He set His face like flint to go to the cross (Isaiah 50:7), and nothing that Satan and his armies could throw across that path would deter Him. Was He a leader? Did He inspire others? Was He able to accomplish great things? Yes, Jesus of Nazareth would certainly have scored high in anyone's "Lion" category.

Did He have any Otter in Him? He was accused by His attackers of being a drunkard and a glutton because He spent so much time at dinners and parties (Luke 5:29-30, 7:34). The very first place Jesus took His disciples was to a wedding party. He attended a number of funerals, but sometimes disrupted them by inviting the former corpse to join the festivities! Through the years of His ministry, He was almost constantly with crowds, small groups, or intimate dinner parties in the homes of friends and acquaintances. He loved embracing children and engaging people from all walks of life in meaningful conversation.

Did He have any Golden Retriever? He was loyal. All the way to the cross. His relationships were deep and enduring. And nothing seemed to get in the way of His deep concern for others. While He was on the way to the cross, staggering from the beatings and loss of blood, He paused to counsel a group of distraught women along the way (Luke 23:26-31). While He was hanging on the cross, enduring unspeakable physical and spiritual agonies, He took time to ensure His mother's social security (John 19:26-27). Even as He was breathing His last, He heard the plea of the felon on the cross next door and invited him Home for dinner (Luke 23:42-43).

Did He display any Beaver? He did things right! He did not turn back from His task until it was thoroughly, eternally accomplished. He is the "*author and perfecter* of our faith, who for the joy set before him endured the cross, scorning its shame, and sat down at the right hand of the throne of God" (Hebrews 12:2).

"People were overwhelmed with amazement. 'He has done everything well,' they said" (Mark 7:37).

If we're serious about having the kind of life that reflects Christ, then we must love people like He did—with a balanced, whole-hearted love.

Are you getting a clear picture of what balanced love looks like? Let's take the time for one more divine portrait.

Centuries ago, God's people had been ripped out of their homeland, and languished in captivity for nearly forty years. When the prophet Isaiah was commanded by God to speak to His people, he sought to prepare them for some wonderful news.

> You who bring good tidings to Zion,
>> go up on a high mountain.
> You who bring good tidings to Jerusalem,
>> lift up your voice with a shout,
>> lift it up, do not be afraid;
>> say to the towns of Judah,
>> "Here is your God!"
> (Isaiah 40:9).

But what did this God look like? How did Isaiah represent Him to a group of people separated from a place of worship for decades?

> See, the Sovereign LORD comes with power,
>> and his arm rules for him (v. 10).

That's a clear picture of God's strength; His mighty arm, like a conquering warrior ruling for Him. Yet that's only one part of the prophet's portrait. Not only did their God have the strength of a lion, He also had the tender sensitivity of a shepherd.

> He tends his flock like a shepherd:
>> He gathers the lambs in his arms
>> and carries them close to his heart;
> he gently leads those that have young
> (v. 11).

If you need a clearer picture of how the Lord Jesus—God in the flesh—reflected this balance, take time to ponder His life in the Gospels. Turn to outstanding books on our Savior from men like our friends Ken Gire and Max Lucado.[2]

### 3. Loving accountability.

During those earlier years of our marriage when I (John) began to struggle with bringing my Otter personality into a Christlike balance, a small group of four or five men made the difference in my life. One man in particular, Doug Childress, took the time to call *my wife* each week to see what progress I was making as a husband and father. And I had the same freedom to do spot-checks on his family life.

This consistent, loving accountability spurred one of the greatest growth periods of my life. I wasn't very wise, but I was wise enough to say, "Guys, I'm out of balance. I want to be more like Christ, and I can't do it without help. I can't do it unless you guys cut through all my Otter talk and hold me accountable to learn and practice some balance in my life." And those guys were just stubborn enough, just loving enough, to take me at my word and do that very thing.

Sometimes, the accountability we need comes in the form of a trained counselor. Diane is an example of someone who found out that God can use a solid, Christian pastor or counselor to help her face crucial issues.

She grew up in a home that seethed with anger and harsh discipline. It left its mark on her. She was often abrasive with others, and especially hard on her husband and children. It took her Golden Retriever husband a long time before he had the courage to put his foot down, but one night, in desperation, he told her that she was either going into counseling—or she was going to move out temporarily.

While she recovered from the shock of his words, he pulled out a list on a legal pad of all the ways she had hurt and offended the children with her cutting words and comments. As he started reading down the list, tears began to form in her eyes.

Diane did seek professional help, and her counselor put her in a small group of women from our church who had also experienced the emotional explosions that took place in alcoholic homes. In the process of meeting with her group—at first at emotional gunpoint—she slowly began to sense the genuine concern and love each woman had for her. If ever there was someone who was loved into God's kingdom, it was Diane. The four women in the group took her on as a personal prayer project, led her to Christ, and now check with her every week to see that the fruits of the Spirit are developing in her life.

Fruits such as peace, patience, and kindness that had to be grafted in and held in place by loving accountability, are now bearing fruit on their own. And by the way, Diane now leads her own group of women...just as angry, just as hard, and just as much in need of accountability and love as she was three years ago.

We all have differences, and some of us even let our strengths be pushed so far out of balance that they become our greatest weaknesses. Wise men and women, however—those open to correction, counsel, and insight—will seek a balanced Christ-like love and find a key to their family's heart.

God loves to help families leave the lights on.

Notes
1. Jim Brawner, *Connections* (Chicago, Ill.: Moody Press, 1992).

2. Ken Gire, *Intimate Moments with the Savior* (Grand Rapids, Mich.: Zondervan Publishers, 1990). Max Lucado, *No Wonder They Call Him the Savior* (Sisters, Ore.: Questar Publishers, 1986).

# Chapter Eight

# UNTYING THE KNOTS OF ANGER

T he man I was counseling seemed a little afraid.

He needed to be a lot afraid.

I (Gary) told him so.

"So you have three teenaged daughters—all beautiful girls— and they're pulling away from you."

"Yes."

"Because of your harshness; because of your anger. Is that right, Jerry?"

"Yes."

"And you're afraid that boys are going to take advantage of that situation—that you are actually pushing your girls into the arms of their boyfriends?"

"Well...yes."

"Jerry, you're exactly right. That's exactly what's going to happen. It's probably happening already."

The words shook him. And he needed shaking. He had been deeply involved in building his own business through most of the girls' growing up years. He worked long hours, weekends, and rarely took vacations. A strong "Lion" temperament type, he liked "laying down the law" and roaring out commands. Tenderness did not seem to be in his vocabulary. As a result, he had filled his daughters' hearts with anger.

"I'm not going to kid with you, Jerry," I told him. "I'm going to flat tell you. You're going to lose your girls. Probably all of them. You don't have a chance unless you start making some massive changes *now*. And even now it may be too late."

I had to speak strongly to him. Gentle words didn't get through to Jerry. But these words did. He remembered them at a crucial moment a few days later.

It was just after a violent argument with his middle daughter, LeeAnn. He had "had his fill" of her interminable telephone conversations with boyfriends. He was going to draw a line and draw it hard. He heard himself shouting at her. He felt his face grow hard with anger.

"NO! That's enough!" he snarled. "Maybe you need *all* your phone privileges revoked. Yeah—maybe you need to stay off that phone completely for a couple weeks. Yeah, I think you do. And that's the way it's gonna be—get used to it!"

Weeping, she ran upstairs. To get away from him. He stood at the bottom of the stairs and watched her. It was all too familiar.

And then for a moment time seem suspended. He seemed to see the scene as though he were watching it on a TV monitor. Angry father standing stiffly at the bottom of the stairs. Weeping, angry daughter *hurrying away from him.*

In a split second all this passed through his mind. In that same split second he thought, *Dear God, I'm doing it again! It's just like Smalley said. I'm pushing her away from me. I have to do something right NOW because I don't want any more anger in her heart.*

So he called to her. Tenderly. In a voice she rarely heard. It was a broken voice; a voice choked with sorrow.

"LeeAnn. LeeAnn, honey. Daddy was so wrong to say what I just said."

She froze on the stairway, her back to him, not believing her ears. *That can't be my daddy talking! I've never heard him talk that way.*

"LeeAnn," the voice went on. "What I just did was so bad. I never should say those kinds of things. I'm so sorry that I do. I'm so sorry for the way I've treated you. I love you, LeeAnn. Would you…could you forgive me?"

She turned, looking at him, eyes shining with tears. And suddenly the distance between them just wasn't there anymore. Suddenly she was down the stairs and in his arms. They held each other for a long time.

Almost too late, Jerry realized what anger was doing to his family. His own hostility had created deep feelings of anger and alienation in his girls. Just in time, he realized he was pushing them into darkness. Just in time, he realized he was digging a dark canyon of separation. Just in time, he built a bridge.

How destructive this bottled up resentment can be! As we've counseled thousands of couples and families, we've observed that anger has many tragic consequences in a marriage or family. Let's look at three of the most deadly.

*1. Anger creates distance.*

Anger almost always creates an unhealthy distance. In Jerry's family, LeeAnn's desire to run out of the room, up the stairs, and into her room was a clear non-verbal signal. She wanted distance between herself and her dad. She couldn't wait to get away from him. If your children are angry with you, they will not be comfortable in your presence. They won't want to do things with you. They won't want you in their rooms. If you are married to an angry man or woman, he or she will try to create distance between you. You may want to get close, but the offended one will pull away. Angry people refuse closeness. Improve the relationship, and they'll sabotage it. Call it black, and they'll call it white—just to keep you at arm's length.

One of our friends told us about growing up with an older brother who had a blistering—but short-lived—temper. The younger boy's first tip-off that he was in trouble was the color of his brother's face. If it went deathly pale, he knew that he would have about a second and a half to vacate the premises before his big brother would grab him in white-hot wrath and shake him like a pit bull mauling a rat. If, however, he could get a jump on his older brother, run like fury, and keep out of his reach for thirty seconds, he was safe. After half a minute his brother would cool off, shrug his shoulders, and forget all about it. In this case, distance was the safest option! (The younger brother eventually joined the track team.)

In most cases, however, distance is a destroyer. It causes husbands and wives and parents and children to drift away from each other. Home becomes little more than a dormitory with hostile roommates.

If you want to be gripped by one of the most heart-piercing stories in all the Bible dealing with this concept, read 2 Samuel 13-18. David, bitterly angry with his son, Absalom, refused to see him for over two years. David's forced separation wounded both of them deeply, to the point that the prince literally went out and started a fire to get his father's attention! Although David finally allowed his son to see him, the terrible hurt and anger had already seared the young man's heart. Absalom would later die in a failed armed rebellion against his dad.

*2. Anger pushes us into darkness.*

The apostle John sketches a striking true-life portrait of what happens as we cling to anger: "Anyone who claims to be in the light but hates his brother is still in the darkness. Whoever loves his brother lives in the light, and there is nothing in him to make him stumble. But whoever hates his brother is in the darkness and walks around in the darkness; he does not know where he is going, because the darkness has blinded him" (1 John 2:9-11).

Have you ever found yourself getting up in the middle of the night in a hotel room—and you can't find a light switch? You need to answer the telephone, turn down the air conditioning, or locate the bathroom, but you find yourself groping in inky blackness—walking into a table, knocking the clock off the nightstand, barking your shin on a chair, or tripping over the shoes you left on the floor. Unresolved anger does that in our lives. It quenches the light in our home like nothing else. It rips away our perspective and throws us into chaos. We don't know where we are. We can't think logically. We don't realize what we're doing to ourselves and those we love. As we blindly lurch and stumble, our families become candidates for serious—possibly permanent—injuries of the heart.

Walking consistently in darkness prevents us from being sensitive or loving toward others. It also kills any interest we have in studying God's Word and puts any desire to pray into the deep-freeze. Further, it robs us of any desire to please and honor Him or to experience His joy, contentment, and peace.

Paul drops a sober warning in Ephesians 4:26-27 when he writes, "In your anger do not sin: Do not let the sun go down while you are still angry, and do not give the devil a foothold." When Satan gets a foothold in a life, it's no laughing matter. Deception and chaos come in the door with him. Unbelievable pain and destruction follow.

We've talked to many people in our counseling who, after years of attending church and seeking God, have still not found peace. After getting to know them better, the major reason for their failure is deep-seated anger. They are unwilling to forgive or seek forgiveness, and as a result they hide secret caches of darkness in their lives—little toxic waste dumps seeping bitterness, gradually poisoning their home.

Both authors of this book have had to acknowledge pockets of unresolved, festering anger at different points in our lives. I (John) grew up in a single-parent home, deeply wounded and angry over the fact that my dad left when I was only three months old. That left my mother to raise three sons—all under three when he left—and it left a father-shaped hole in my heart.

I can remember hating him during the years when I was going to father/son banquets with a neighbor's dad, and looking up from the football field and seeing all the other players' dads in the stands. But then I became a Christian, and I knew I couldn't hate him any more. So I just "intensely disliked" him. Same emotions, different words, same consequence of darkness. For years I was unwilling to let go of my anger.

While my father was an angry ex-marine, Gary grew up in a home with an angry merchant marine. His father was always angry, constantly belittling and devaluing other members of the family.

Anger from a parent is like a can of red paint spraying out of his or her mouth. It sprays all over the kids, leaving a sticky mess that can take years to clean off. At different points, both of us had to admit our bitter anger, forgive our fathers, and ask God to wash the darkness out of our hearts—before we spread it to our own families.

This veil of darkness so blinds many angry men and women that they don't "wake up" to the havoc they've wrought in a home until the very walls of the family come crashing down. The anger they have spewed out at members of their family has doubled back and blinded them to God's love and that of others.

We've come to realize that no matter how hard we work on the relational "glue" to bond each of our families together, anger is like fingernail polish remover that instantly dissolves that bonding. It trickles into the emotional heart of a relationship, chilling feelings of warmth or attachment.

No wonder Paul calls dads aside for a moment in Ephesians 6:4 (NASB) and says, "Fathers, do not provoke your children to anger." Again, in Colossians 3:21, the apostle looks parents eyeball to eyeball and warns, "Do not embitter your children, or they will become discouraged."

*3. Anger ties us in knots.*

Like few other emotions, anger restricts and binds us, tying us in internal knots. Forgiveness, on the other hand, sets us free from those bonds, untying the knots that hold us captive. The Lord Jesus gives us a powerful word picture of forgiveness in Luke 6:37, when He says, "Forgive, and you will be forgiven." The word He uses for "forgive" in the original language literally means *to release fully, to unbind,* or *to let go.* It is the only time in all the New Testament that this word is translated "forgive." In every other instance, it means "release" or "free," as when Lazarus came out of the tomb bound hand and foot in grave clothes, and Jesus said, "*Unbind* him, and let him go" (John 11:44, NASB).

Like rope tied around our feet or hands, anger hinders and hampers us. Children who grow up embittered and angry are handcuffed and hobbled, prevented from discovering their potential. Seeking their forgiveness is like releasing them from tight ropes that bite into their lives and cut off life-giving circulation.

After witnessing first-hand the devastation anger can produce in a family, we have identified five crucial attitudes—not steps—that can drain even long-held anger out of a person's heart and life.

### FIVE ATTITUDES TO UNTIE A PERSON'S ANGER KNOTS

*1. Become soft and tender with the person.*

Proverbs says, "A gentle answer turns away wrath" (Proverbs 15:1). When Jerry began to speak tenderly to his daughter, it literally halted her in the act of running away. Things began to turn around when his voice softened along with his spirit. His attitude and voice said he cared about her. Sometimes softness alone can melt an anger-hardened heart.

*2. Understand, as much as possible, what the other person has endured.*

As hard as it was for a macho type like Jerry, he humbled himself in front of his daughter and forced himself to see things from her point of view. It *would* be difficult to live with a harsh father who showed so little care and tenderness. It *would* be frustrating and embarrassing to have someone yell at you while you were on the phone. It *would* be crushing to look up and see your father's face contorted with anger.

*3. Admit the person has been wounded, and be sure to admit any wrong in provoking that hurt.*

"LeeAnn," Jerry had said. "What I just did was so bad. I never should say those kinds of things. I'm so sorry that I do. I'm so sorry for the way I've treated you."

As a parent (or a spouse), those can be some of the most difficult words we will ever speak. Jim Brauner, our Kannakuk friend, did a survey of several thousand high school students coming through their summer camp. Do you know what he found? The number one complaint teenagers voiced about their parents could be summed up in five words: "They never say 'I'm sorry.' "

But as it did with LeeAnn, those words—when spoken with deep sincerity—can loosen even the hardest knots of anger. Admitting we are wrong (when we clearly are) is like turning the key on a pair of too-tight handcuffs. The release and relief can be almost immediate.

Sometimes we may not think we are wrong, but our attitude may be. Or, it may be the way we've done something that's offensive. If my spirit is critical and angry when I tell my child about a legitimate problem, I'm still wrong.

James had it right when he wrote, "…man's anger [or woman's anger] does not bring about the righteous life that God desires" (James 1:20). Stopping short of admitting we were wrong leaves a dangerous gap between you and your child or mate that may not mend quickly—or at all.

*4. Seek forgiveness—and trust God for their response.*

In that incredibly important moment at the bottom of the stairway, Jerry spoke the best words he could have used. "I'm so sorry for the way I've treated you. I love you, LeeAnn. Would you…could you forgive me?"

We've used words like these with our own families: "Could you forgive me? I know I've let you down again and again. I know I don't deserve your forgiveness, but I'm still asking for it." Or, "I don't want you all tied up in knots because of what I've said or the way I've acted. I know I have a long way to go before I get this area of my life straightened around, but I love you very much, and I ask you to forgive me. Will you forgive me?"

Try to get a positive response from the person before you turn away, but if you need to, start with the first loving attitude of being soft and work your way back to forgiveness. Remember, too, *don't just respond to your loved one's words.* If you've deeply hurt someone, that person may say something in retaliation to hurt you.

For many people, men in particular, hearing sharp words can set off a defensive reaction, even another round of battle. But those men or women who are wise enough to untie the anger knots in another's heart have to learn to listen beyond the words—to the hurt feelings behind the emotional outburst. There is tension in some of those knots. Untying them sometimes releases some of the negative feelings that have been held in check. Your focus should be on untying the knots and releasing the anger—even if it gets uncomfortable for you.

However, as you seek to resolve anger with another person, keep trusting God for the strength to do what's right regardless of that person's response.

Over twenty years ago during my college years, I (John) became deeply convicted about my relationship with my father. It was he who had walked out on me, my brothers, and my mother. It was he who had never come to any of our football games or spoken a single word of affirmation. But I realized that it was *me* who was losing sleep over it, not him. While the anger in his life had certainly tied him in knots, I was repeating a pattern of his I didn't want to follow.

I can remember like yesterday calling and taking my father out to a nice seafood restaurant. As we sat at the table that night, I asked his forgiveness for being angry at him—and even for hating him at times. As a non-Christian, he shrugged off my attempt to seek forgiveness, and I can't say that he walked away from the table any different than when he came in.

But I did.

From that awkward hour in a restaurant booth, my life has been different for over twenty years. Not because he changed, but because I had.

We can't take responsibility for another person's acceptance of our apology or forgiveness. But we can persist in doing what is right, and humbly admit our own knots of anger that can dramatically effect our own lives.

### 5. Touch the person gently.

When the anger had drained out of LeeAnn's spirit, she flew down the stairs into her father's arms. The physical and emotional distance between them was bridged in an instant. But it's not always that easy.

If you try to touch someone with a spirit knotted in anger, you will find out just how deep the hurt is. The first response may very well be a stiffening or a pulling away. But persistent softness expressed in meaningful touches, like the gentle massage of a knotted muscle, can go a long way toward draining anger and negative feelings.

When you talk to many older couples suddenly facing the prospect of an empty nest, you hear the same comment repeated again and again. "Enjoy the kids while you can, because the time flies by! They grew up so fast we can hardly believe it."

Since our parenting time is so brief, let's not allow precious days and weeks and months to be shadowed by the bitterness and separation of unresolved anger. With God's help, let's take the initiative to untie the knots...while we still can.

# RESOLVING CONFLICT

It was a blended family that wasn't blending.

The kids were taking sides, mostly against Dad.

His frustration escalated daily, making him even harder to live with than before (when it wasn't easy). The stress under that Tucson, Arizona, roof mounted to nightmare proportions.

An alarmed friend of the couple strongly suggested they attend one of our "Love Is a Decision" seminars being held in Phoenix that weekend. As a last resort, they decided to make the two hour drive and attend.

They almost never made it.

Round One of their sharpest argument yet began nine miles out of town on I-10 just past the Maranna exit.

Round Two took them a few more miles down the interstate.

The stress grew mile by mile as the argument exploded into a savage shouting match.

*That sinks it,* the husband thought. *I'm not going to any "love" seminar with this woman. I've had it with this relationship. I'm turning around.*

He began looking for the next exit, relishing the dramatic prospects of a sharp turn, squealing tires, and a fast retreat to Tucson. Even as his eyes scanned the road ahead, however, a dim voice inside told him that an exit from the freeway at that point would be mean an exit from his marriage.

And by the way...where in the world *were* the exits?

He had just driven by the Toltec exit, but before the next one he drove five miles, ten miles, fifteen miles, *twenty miles.* No exits. No turn-arounds. Nothing! Wouldn't you know it? They happened to be on a twenty-two-mile stretch of freeway where there simply weren't any opportunities to turn back!

By the time he'd driven the twenty-two miles, they were nearing Casa Grande and were past the point of no return. So with a sense of weary resignation he thought, *Well, we're already this close. May as well go through with the thing.*

In His grace and kindness, God had not allowed them to turn back on their decision to seek help for their floundering family. They attended the seminar, and the concepts and relationship skills they learned that weekend brought their marriage out of the emergency lane. It was one of the most dramatic marriage and family transformations we had ever seen in our ministry.

Among the most helpful things they learned that weekend were several crucial keys to resolving conflict in a family. Within the next few pages, let's take a brief look at a few of the concepts that kept this Tucson couple from taking an early exit from their marriage and put them "on the road" to family harmony.

### THREE LEVELS OF CONFLICT

To understand how we can keep disagreements from becoming destructive, let's look at an imaginary couple with a not-so-imaginary money problem.

At first it looks like good news. Bill discovers that a barely-remembered-but-now-highly-valued great aunt has passed away and left him $22,000. Fine woman! He can almost visualize her saintly face.

The sudden cash windfall isn't the problem. The problem comes in determining what to *do* with the money. Bill has a ready answer. He's had his eye on a forest green Ford Explorer in the parking lot at work. One of his co-workers can't keep up the payments on the four-wheel-drive wonder, and is willing to sacrifice it. Just a few days before, buying the vehicle was little more than a pleasant dream. Now...well suddenly, it is a dream within reach. Bill starts salivating just thinking about getting behind the wheel.

The ISSUE surfaces when Bill's practical-minded wife, Barb, questions putting the money into a car instead of *saving* it. After all, she reasons, Bill knows they have virtually nothing in the bank. What would happen in an emergency? What would they fall back on? Barb would feel more peace of mind if she knew they had a big chunk of that inheritance safely tucked away in a certificate of deposit, quietly gaining interest and providing a comforting blanket of security.

With Bill's Explorer dreams suddenly galloping out of reach, he jumps into the argument. Barb *knows* how much he wants that Explorer. Their Toyota has nearly seventy thousand miles on it. They could do more camping as a family with a four-wheel drive rig (and camping is such a great family activity). He could *never* get that kind of price on that kind of Explorer again. And besides all that, it was *his* great aunt who passed away. Surely she had his happiness in mind when she left him the money. Barb wouldn't want to frustrate an old woman's last wish, would she?

You get the idea. The ISSUE is the first level of conflict. If Bill and Barb can keep it on the ISSUE level, discussing the merits of each position and thinking through possible compromises, the tension could actually be constructive rather than destructive.

The next level of conflict, however, can be very hurtful. Seeing his fantasy suddenly frustrated by his wife's inexplicable attack of caution, an angry Bill leaves off attacking the ISSUE and begins attacking the PERSON. If Barb were *really* a caring wife, she would want her husband to be happy. If she weren't always thinking about herself, she would realize this was a chance in a lifetime for him to own the kind of car he had wanted since he was a teenager.

Barb, in turn, could argue that if Bill were *really* a sensitive husband, then *he* would realize they needed a little nest egg. And maybe if he had been more responsible with their money to begin with, they wouldn't be in such a financial bind all the time.

They still haven't solved the ISSUE, and now they are locked in an attack on the PERSON of their spouse. If nothing changes, they will move on to a third step; the most destructive and dangerous level of the conflict. In the third level, they begin to question the RELATIONSHIP. They are one step away from the cliff.

Either to themselves or out loud, they begin to say things like, *If these are the kinds of issues we're facing and this is the kind of person I'm living with, then what am I doing in this relationship?*

The tragic part of allowing an argument to escalate to this third level is that if a person entertains these thoughts for long, almost every problem in the relationship immediately jumps from the ISSUE level to the RELATIONSHIP level and skips level two! In other words, that's when squeezing the toothpaste tube in the wrong place instantly becomes grounds for divorce.

Couples who want to back away from this deadly precipice must learn to keep their arguments on the ground floor—at the *issue* level. At this level, a couple is focusing on the problem itself and attempting to find ways to solve it. Ask yourself a difficult question. At what level do you stop in disagreeing with your spouse? Better yet, ask your wife or husband at what level *he* or *she* thinks you stop.

In our counseling, we get couples to commit themselves to not going beyond level two. Actually, we try to persuade them to stay at level one. Whenever they find themselves at level three, that's when warning lights ought to be going off.

Couples who consistently find themselves at level three need to let this be the signal to send them to competent Christian counseling…before asking the wrong questions leads them to disastrously wrong answers.

## SAYING HARD WORDS IN A SOFT WAY

Another skill our real-life couple from Tucson learned at the "Love Is a Decision" seminar was how to voice a hard thing in a soft way through the use of emotional word pictures. An emotional word picture is a communication tool that reaches both the mind and the heart. It causes another person to not just hear our words, but to actually *experience* them. This productive skill is helping thousands of families to communicate deeply-felt concerns and ideas in a way that "breaks through" resistant attitudes and responses.

The Scripture contains countless word pictures. Do you remember the story of the prophet Nathan confronting King David over his dual sins of adultery and murder? If Nathan had simply walked into David's presence and laid the charges on him, he might have walked out of the room with his head under his arm. Instead of confronting the king head-on, he slipped in through the back door with a story of a poor man, a fluffy pet lamb, and a cruel and greedy rancher. With David's emotions and sense of justice fully engaged, Nathan had only to spring the punch line to bring the king to his knees.

It needn't be that dramatic. We were doing a radio call-in program in the Pacific Northwest when a lady phoned in with a less sensational but still encouraging success story. She had been upset because of her husband's harshness toward their two young boys. He worked a graveyard shift and came home to sleep while the boys, ages eight and six, were in school. About the time he would wake up, the boys would arrive home for the day. This is where the problem occurred.

The two rambunctious boys would come piling off the school bus and burst excitedly through the front door, ready to throw off the rigors of the classroom, grab a snack, and have some fun. Their father, however, felt the need for a quiet "interval" after pulling himself out of bed. The yelling and laughing and chasing around made him angry. Didn't those darned kids know that he worked all night? Couldn't a man have a few minutes of quiet in his own home to sip a cup of coffee and get his eyes open?

As a result, he was becoming increasingly severe with his sons, clamping down on them as soon as they came in through the door. The mom felt sorry for the boys, who after all were only being boys, and tried to stick up for them. It wasn't as though they were waking him up; he was usually up by then anyway. Was it reasonable for him to demand absolute peace and quiet? This would inevitably tangle Mom and Dad in an argument, and the whole family began to suffer from the strain.

That was when this lady decided to try an emotional word picture with her husband. She knew he was an avid Seattle Seahawk football fan. He had season tickets to the games and lived for those Sunday gridiron contests.

One afternoon before the kids got home he sat down at the kitchen table for his coffee and toast. Looking down at his plate, he was surprised to see his season tickets rather than two slices of buttered wheat toast.

"What's this?" he mumbled.

"Those are your Seahawk tickets, dear," she said.

"I know *that*, but what are they doing here?"

"Well…I know there's a game coming up. Aren't the Seahawks playing Denver this Sunday?"

"You bet! That's the game I've been waiting on for a year. It's gonna be great. But what are my tickets doing here on the table?"

"Oh, just to remind me. Well, I don't know how to tell you this…"

"Tell me what?"

"About the Seahawks."

"What about the Seahawks?"

"Well—I just heard something on the radio that I know is going to upset you."

"About the game? Did someone get injured or something?"

"No. It's just about the new rule the NFL is going to enforce on crowd noise. You know how loud it is in the Kingdome. All that yelling and screaming. The opposing quarterbacks can't even hear themselves calling signals."

"What about it?"

"Well—they had to do something about Seattle. They're not going to let Seattle fans yell at the games any more."

"Aw, get outta here!"

"Well—it's just that the new NFL rule says…"

"Gimme a break! That's why you go to football games! I bought my tickets, that's my team, and if I wanna yell, I'm gonna yell! That's my part of the stadium, I paid for it, and they're not gonna stop me."

"Well, honey, guess what? I was just kidding."

"Awww, I knew you were anyway."

"But let me tell you why I did that." And then she handed him two other "tickets" she had carefully made to look like Seahawks tickets. He stared at them uncomprehendingly. The "tickets" bore the names of his two boys.

She sat down beside him. "Honey, maybe you haven't thought about it, but our two boys have a ticket to live in this home. And when you're so hard on them—for just acting like little boys—well, that would be just like someone saying you could go to the Kingdome but couldn't cheer for your team. No—I agree—the boys don't need to be out of control and screaming at the top of their lungs in the house, and I've talked to them about that. But this is their Kingdome and you can't expect them to act like mice. Not at their age and not at their energy level."

Suddenly that father got a clear picture of what he was doing to his kids. Rather than being offended, he took the message to heart. Instead of attacking him as a PERSON or questioning their RELATIONSHIP, she focused on the ISSUE in a way that helped him picture the problem in a new way.

## BRINGING EVERYONE ON BOARD

We've been speaking about resolving conflict between spouses, which is critical for family harmony. But it's also important to bring the rest of the family into the process. Disregarding the children's wishes and feelings in major family decisions—such as a cross-country move—can have damaging consequences.

A counselee of mine (John's) recently told me of being suddenly uprooted at the age of fourteen. She lived with her divorced mom and her mom's live-in boyfriend. Despite the difficult home situation, this resilient teenager enjoyed an extensive network of support and encouragement through teachers, neighbors, and close friends. One evening, however, her mom and the boyfriend came to her and said, "Pack your stuff and get it into the car. We're moving to a different state. *Tonight.*"

They were ducking town to avoid paying a stack of bills. Since the move was secretive, they would not allow this heartbroken girl to call a single friend to say goodbye. By midnight they were on the road.

That teenager is now forty years old and finds it almost impossible to bond with *anyone*—her husband, her children, her neighbors. The memory of that midnight move tied such a knot in her life that to this day she struggles to loosen its grip.

We recommend that families try to *resolve* an issue in a way that brings mutual satisfaction to everyone rather than forcing a compromise that no one is really happy with. One method we've recommended for years is a simple fact-gathering process that results in a decision-making chart on major family issues.

If it's an important decision—What car should we buy? What home should we buy? Should we try a different church? Should we move?—we suggest that the family take a piece of paper and make a couple of lists. First, list all the reasons, pro and con, for making a change. Next, list all the reasons, pro and con, for *not* doing it. Third, evaluate each reason. Will the decision have lasting effects? Is the reason selfish, or will it help others? What do we think God would have us do, and why?

Bring the children in on this process, even the little ones as they are able, because that gives them ownership in the decision. We recommend that families never move from one city to another unless the children have the opportunity to voice their fears, desires, and hopes. We've seen too much anger in our counseling created by parents who simply ran roughshod over the feelings and opinions of their children.

If a decision touches the kids *in any way*, at least give them the opportunity to give their input. Get it down on a piece of paper so that everyone can see their opinions and wishes are being taken into consideration.

Whenever possible, don't go forward with a major decision until you've had a chance to get all the relevant information on the table, hear everyone's opinions, and gain a family consensus.

## COMBAT CONFLICT BY GOING ON THE OFFENSIVE

Every football season, one thousand television announcers and ten thousand coaches will echo an overused gridiron axiom: the best offense is a good defense. And while it's overused on call-in sports shows, the idea is underused in too many families.

If you're serious about defeating the arguments and problems that can crop up around any home, try seasoning each day with a liberal sprinkling of praise. Can't think of anything to say to your child or spouse? Why not copy these words on your heart, and use them every day.

Are these words consistently echoing off the wall in your home? If so, we can almost guarantee that the conflict level is down to the "occasional" range.

• I'm proud of you • Way to go • Bingo—you did it • Magnificent • I knew you could do it • What a good helper • You're very special to me • I trust you • What a treasure you are • Hooray for you • Beautiful work • You're a real trooper • Well done • That's so creative • You make my day • You're a joy • Give me a big hug • You're such a good listener • You figured it out • I love you • You're so responsible • You remembered • You're the best • You sure tried hard • I have to hand it to you • I couldn't be prouder of you • You light up my day • My buttons are popping off • I'm praying for you • You're wonderful • I'm with you all the way •

We can't think of a better way to leave the lights on in your home than going on the offensive to affirm and value your loved ones. Just think how the Lord Jesus went on the offensive for us!

Already we have the love of God flooding through our hearts by the Holy Spirit given to us. And we can see that it was at the very time that we were powerless to help ourselves that Christ died for sinful men. In human experience it is a rare thing for one man to give his life for another, even if the latter be a good man, though there have been a few who have had the courage to do it. Yet the proof of God's amazing love is this: that it was while we were sinners that Christ died for us (Romans 5:5-8, Phillips).

## SLOW DOWN TO GET THE FACTS

When you boil down a lot of destructive family arguments, what you often find is a simple lack of facts. The conflict begins when an individual sees something that bothers him and then draws a conclusion. What he *thinks* he sees may not be true at all.

There's nothing new about this advice. The Lord's brother, James, jotted it down for a group of early Christians nearly two millennia ago. Guess what? They had family conflicts, too. And Pastor James had a little counsel that twenty decades of human experience and two million psychologists have never improved upon.

"My dear brothers, take note of this: Everyone should be quick to listen, slow to speak and slow to become angry" (James 1:19).

Now *that's* what we call profound!

*Chapter      Ten*

# THE GLUE THAT BONDS A FAMILY

They sat on a log near the lakeside, sipping Pepsi and nibbling beef jerky and granola bars. Funny how such simple cuisine can taste so good after a long hike.

Ron, Karen, and their two children had been camping in the Oregon mountains. Leaving their campsite that morning, they decided to trek into an isolated mountain lake for a picnic lunch. Nine-year-old Ross and six-year-old Jenny kept up a pretty good pace, but they still consumed over ninety minutes (and a bag and a half of trail mix) to reach their destination.

Standing beside the quiet lake after lunch, the children were balancing on some rocks when the family's adventure took a sudden, jarring turn. Jenny's sneakers slipped out from under her and—unable to catch herself with her hands on the sharp lava rock—she tumbled full-force onto her forehead.

Head wounds being what they are, there was a lot of blood and crying and everyone was scared and shaken. With his bandaged girl clinging

115

limply to his back, Ron led the return journey to the car in just forty-five minutes, gently murmuring all the words of encouragement he could think of.

An hour after they reached the car, Jenny was resting comfortably in an emergency room with ten stitches in her forehead but no permanent harm. Ron didn't realize how the incident had bonded him with his daughter until several months later. The rambunctious little girl had yet another fall—this time on the playground—badly bruising her thigh. As he was piggy-backing her to the car she leaned over and whispered in his ear, *"Doesn't this seem familiar?"*

They both laughed despite the new injury. They had weathered a crisis together, these two, and somehow the hurts and jolts would never seem quite so threatening...if they faced them together.

That's the crazy, wonderful thing about facing difficulties together as a family. It's the family that *does* things together—enduring the inevitable breakdowns, foul-ups, contusions, concussions, and minor disasters—that ends up being known as a "close family."

We speak to thousands of couples and families annually. Over the years, whenever we spot a noticeably close, happy family in the audience, we try to interview the family members separately. We ask them, "What do you think is the main reason you are all so close and happy?" With few exceptions, we hear the same answer over and over. "We do a lot of things together."

Some elaborate, saying, "We've made a commitment to spend quality *and* quantity time together. We have separate interests, but we make sure we regularly do things together as a family."

*1. Shared experiences—with the potential for shared trials—is the glue that bonds a family.*

It isn't just talking that draws people together. Experts on friendship tell us that people don't become close friends by talking; they become close by doing things together.

In his book *The Four Loves*, C. S. Lewis talks about *phileo*, the "friendship" or "brotherly" kind of love. Friendship, Lewis writes, is what happens in the context of doing something together. Two women—casual acquaintances—decide to serve on a PTA committee. In the process of voicing mutual concerns, tip-toeing through a bureaucratic minefield, hammering out an action plan, and sweating through a public presentation, they discover they've become good friends. They didn't set out to find friendship. It simply overtook them in the process of working shoulder to shoulder toward a common goal.

Sometimes two guys who were best buddies in college get together with their wives in later years and try to rekindle the old friendship. Often the effort fails. The simple determination "we're going to be friends" doesn't provide enough glue to cement the couples together. Real relationship glue is a byproduct of shared experiences…even negative ones!

I (John) can vouch for that as I look back on a trip I made with my family several years ago to speak at Pine Cove, one of the top family camp centers in the country.

Pine Cove is just the right size for a great camping experience and boasts one of the most friendly and helpful staffs I've ever seen. We were all looking forward to the bonding that would take place as we canoed and swam and sang together in the evenings. Little did I know, however, that the real bonding would happen before we ever got to camp!

The night before we were to leave for camp, my father—with whom I had tried to stay in contact over the years—was scheduled for exploratory surgery. Everything turned out fine, but I was up all night at the hospital making sure he was all right and that the tests were successful. I screeched into the driveway just as dawn was breaking and the rest of the family was taking showers, getting dressed, eating breakfast, and cramming those last few "important" items into suitcases already about to explode.

That's when our oldest daughter, Kari, in an effort to "help Mommy pack," reached out and grabbed a plugged-in curling iron—right by the heating element.

Our precious little one's screams were enough to melt the hardest parent's heart. In a heartbeat, we were headed back to the hospital to see what degree burns we were faced with—and whether we'd be going to camp at all!

We did finally end up at Pine Cove (Kari clinging to her "Boo Boo Bunny" they gave her at the hospital and getting massive sympathy from everyone who saw her bandaged hand) and to this day we talk about how much the incident bonded us to each other and to Pine Cove.

Time and again, Cindy and I have found that it's often what happens on the way to a special outing that brings the best memories and provokes the greatest laughs.

• Like the time on the airliner when I spilled a full glass of apple juice over Cindy and Kari. Then, after apologizing to the girls, going after some towels, and mopping up the sticky mess, I got a fresh, brimming glass of apple juice from the sympathetic flight attendant *and did it again!* They finally asked the attendant if they could sit in a different row!

• Or when our rental car broke down on the freeway—halfway to Disneyland.

• Or how my little girl and I got carried away bouncing on the motel bed one night, incurring the wrath of a crabby older couple in the next room who began yelling and banging on the walls.

• Or how that one massive wave in an otherwise calm sea "crept up" behind Kari on the beach and flattened her at the very moment Daddy was posing her for the perfect picture.

None of us would plan traumas just to enhance family togetherness. But if your family is anything like the Smalleys or Trents, you don't have to plan them. They just happen! Active families who do things together inevitably experience a few chuck-holes, detours, and fender-benders in their journeys. For some reason I (Gary) haven't yet figured out, in the Smalley household, these mini-disasters often involved my son Greg.

Not long ago Greg said to me, "Dad, for some reason I trust you. Always have and probably always will. But I don't know what it is about you. You can get me into the most awful predicaments!" Maybe he was thinking back to several summers ago when we made the rope swing. We were staying in a cabin near the big lake in Branson, Missouri. My idea of a great water game is to tie a rope to an overhanging tree branch near the bank and swing Tarzan-style way out over the water, riding the momentum to a cannon-ball splashdown.

We had the rope and I had already scouted out the perfect tree limb. It was big and thick and about thirty feet off the ground.

"Hey, Greg!" I called. "Look at that limb. Is that perfect, or what?"

Greg peered doubtfully at the lofty branch. "Gee, I dunno, Dad. That's a long way up there. High above the bank. And look at this dirt— it's hard as a rock. Besides, how would someone get up there?"

That was the opening I'd been waiting for. "Hey, it's no problem. Look at that big vine going up the tree. You're real strong—a weight lifter. You could crawl up that vine easy—just like climbing a rope in football practice. Then you could haul yourself up on the limb and I'll throw you a saw. All you have to do is saw off the vine—because it would be in our way when we wanted to swing—and then I'll throw the rope up to you and you can tie it around the limb with this chain. You can do the whole thing and then just climb down the rope! What could be easier?"

He debated with himself for a moment, probably remembering some of my earlier "easy" schemes, and then took the plunge. After all, his dad had confidence in him. "Yeah, I guess I could do that," he said.

He made it all the way to the top of the vine, while Michael and I shouted encouragement from below. Next he scrambled to a sitting position on the limb, and after about ten tries, caught the little saw I threw him from the ground. He dutifully sawed off the vine, wrapped the chain around the limb, and tied the rope around it.

Meanwhile, I tied a piece of wood to the bottom of the rope and our Wild-Man-of-Missouri rope swing was ready for action.

"Okay, Greg," I shouted up to him, "you can come down now."

The voice coming down to me from the leafy heights sounded unsure of itself.

"Uh, Dad…are you sure I can grip this thing?"

"No problem," I told him. "Just wrap your leg round the rope to slow your slide and go for it!"

Greg crawled down the chain, gripped the rope…and then lost his nerve. Panic crept into his voice.

"Dad! I don't think I can come down the rope—and I don't think I can get back up on the limb again! What am I gonna do? DAD! I'm— I'm starting to lose my grip!"

"Just go for it Greg! Do it before your strength runs out. You've gotta do it! Put your leg around the rope and come down!"

Greg came down. He shot suddenly down the rope like a fireman on a greased pole. He not only burned his leg, he hit the hard ground like a bag of cement. *WHUNK!* To make matters worse, no one had noticed that the people who had cleared the field had cut bamboo, leaving six-inch shoots sticking out of the ground like little daggers.

I stood over my son's prone figure and said in my most affirming voice, "Greg, geee, you did it!"

"Dad," he said, staring into the hard Missouri dirt, "just don't talk to me for awhile, okay?"

It was about half-an-hour before he would even speak to me, and another half-hour before he was able to laugh about it. And you know, we've been laughing about it ever since. We both look back on that incident as a bonding experience, though he still says, "Can you *believe* I let you talk me into these things? It's happened all my life! When am I going to learn?"

Most of the time, being neck-deep in a crisis doesn't find us saying, "Isn't this great? We're all feeling so close right now!" Normally, it gets tense, and we have to choke back words of anger or frustration. The secret is how we'll feel later. In most cases it takes a couple of weeks for the "glue" of a shared predicament to take place. Once set, though, it's usually so tight that virtually nothing can tear the memory away from us.

What kind of a "memory book" are you writing together as a family? Could your little tribe spend an evening of sharing and laughter saying, "Remember when..."? Does your book contain any stories that get better with the telling? Do the pages have vivid color pictures of crazy dilemmas, rainy nights in a tent, tipped canoes, water slides, rope burns long healed, and unforgettable shared experiences? Or is it all set in straight, gray, predictable type? *Whichever way it goes, your family story can only be written once!*

Years ago I (Gary) had a sad conversation with a father who wished he could go back and rewrite his own family's memory book. His comments have helped fuel my family activity wagon over the years. This man sadly admitted that when he and his children meet nowadays for a rare get-together, they hardly have a thing to talk about.

"It's a sickening experience," he said, "to have your children come back home for a visit and you have nothing in common." Funny anecdotes were rare in that family story, and there were few pictures to brighten the monotonous text. His wife had her women's clubs, he had his men's clubs, and the children had their activities. They grew apart in separate worlds.

"Now that my wife and I are alone, we have very little in common," he sighed. "We're two lonely people lost in our five bedroom house."

You can't schedule shared family crises, but you can—and must—schedule family together times. And that's our next point.

*2. Make sure family activities get high priority on your yearly schedule.*

If you plan to add vivid color pictures to your family memory book, it will only be because you and your spouse sit down with a calendar and sharp pencil and make it happen. There will be plenty of "good" and "pressing" reasons to put off a family vacation or camping trip. When the children get older, family activities run into stiff competition from team sports, club activities, and church youth group trips. Nevertheless, you must decide together as a family that shared experiences are a priority and you will not allow them to get squeezed out of the schedule.

We suggest that moms and dads set aside an evening each month to look ahead and discuss the next family adventure—whether it's an in-town picnic, a weekend get-away, or that once-a-year extended vacation.

*3. Watch for key one-on-one opportunities to bond with your children.*

I (Gary) remember so well the week I took Kari, then just nine years old, on a ministry trip with me. Something happened during those seven days that I can't explain. Some inexplicable wall that had grown between us melted away—and has never returned.

She was there in my seminars, handing out materials and smiling encouragement to me from the front row. We stayed together with a family in an old white farmhouse in rural Washington state. We drove through the little town where I grew up and saw some of the places where I used to play as a boy. We walked along a beach by the wide Columbia River, picking up driftwood and watching the ships and barges glide by in the distance.

As we drove the many miles between seminars, we talked about a hundred different things. At other times we didn't talk at all; it was enough just being together. Some of the most precious pictures in my whole memory book grew out of that week. And the whole thing never would have happened if my wise wife hadn't suggested I maximize the time with a little girl I didn't know nearly well enough.

Over the years, Kari and I have preserved that intimate father-daughter relationship by going out together for frozen yogurt, talking about things that are important to each of us. Others we know have worked alongside their children serving Thanksgiving dinners at a local Salvation Army shelter, or visiting the elderly in a retirement home. Whatever the activity, whether going into the hills to cut firewood, driving to the office on Saturday to pick up a computer printout, or walking to the corner convenience store for a newspaper *take one of your kids along*. Make the most of every opportunity, realizing that those opportunities are finite and may never be repeated.

It wouldn't take long these days to write a book on "Fifty Thousand Ways to Fragment a Family." Just get out your tape recorder and interview a few of your neighbors, golf partners, co-workers, and relatives. Lots of people could fill the pages in that sort of book.

There's no end to bitterness. There's no shortage of tears, loneliness, and alienation. It's no great task to blow a family into pieces...or allow each member to drift away into distant, unrecoverable orbits. But bonding a family together, now...creating indelible memories of shared troubles, laughter, and mutual encouragement...well, that's the kind of book *we* would rather read in our old age when all the kids have left home.

We have a hunch you would, too.

# Chapter Eleven

# HOW TO HELP YOUR FAMILY IMPROVE

N obody talked about Grandfather.

It was an unspoken, ironclad rule.

The circumstances of his passing were a family matter, and family matters were private. Period. You didn't bring up someone else's problems, and you *certainly* didn't discuss your own.

Grandfather had become ill with tuberculosis; that much the family knew. This was back in the early 1950s and there were fewer treatment options for TB. Some folks went into a "home" to convalesce. Others chose to stay in their own residence and ride out the disease.

Grandfather chose what he considered the "manly" option. He set his affairs in order, drove his pickup into a lonely canyon in the desert, took out his twelve-gauge, and shot himself.

Then…it was as if he had never existed. His name never came up again. No one spoke of the incident for nearly fourteen years.

Years after that suicide, Grandfather's oldest son strongly suspected he was developing cancer of the colon. An initial diagnosis pointed in that direction. Like his father before him, he stoically determined that he "should not be a burden," went off to a secluded place, and took *his* own life.

Another family secret. No one talked about it. Even when the autopsy revealed that this man in his early forties didn't have cancer at all. The diagnosis had been premature—and incorrect.

Scarcely months later, another brother thought he had contracted a debilitating disease. Would he keep this unspoken, deadly family custom? He planned on it...but then something happened that stopped his hand just in time.

When news of this man's illness came to light, pressure in the family built like steam trapped in a boiler. What in the world was going on? Who was going to be next? Lives were at stake. *Yet no one was willing to speak. No one was willing to break a multi-generational code of silence— even when it was killing them.* No one, that is, until the daughter of this man secretly came to me (John) for counseling.

She was the only member of the clan with the courage to admit that something was seriously wrong—deadly wrong—in her family. They needed help. They needed correction. And she was the only one wise enough to acknowledge it.

When this terrible "family secret" finally came to light in a confrontation with her family, it threw them into a tailspin. Being honest for the first time in years, however, was the very thing that finally brought them out of the darkness and into the freedom of God's light. One woman in a disturbed family had the courage to seek help, and it ended up keeping her own father from fulfilling a terrible legacy.

*Only the wise seek correction.* That biblical idea may not get much airtime in today's culture, but the timeless Word of God declares it over and over. Just look at this sampling from the pen of Solomon:

*"He who heeds discipline shows the way to life, but whoever ignores correction leads others astray."*

*"Whoever loves discipline loves knowledge, but he who hates correction is stupid."*

*"He who ignores discipline comes to poverty and shame, but whoever heeds correction is honored."*

*"Whoever heeds correction shows prudence."*

*"Stern discipline awaits him who leaves the path; he who hates correction will die."*

*"A mocker resents correction; he will not consult the wise."*

*"He who ignores discipline despises himself, but whoever heeds correction gains understanding."*

*(Proverbs 10:17; 12:1; 13:18; 15:5,10,12,32.)*

## HOW DO YOU SPELL WISDOM?

Only the wise seek and love correction. Only the wise love those who correct them. Is it normal for a person to want correction? Does it feel natural to like correction? No. But only the wise know that it's wise. They *choose* to be wise by seeking it out.

The wisest companies in the world have evaluation forms that invite correction from their customers. You see it in all the finest restaurants, hotels, and airlines.

"Please help us improve!"

"Tell us how we're doing!"

"Talk back to us!"

"How's our service?"

"How's my driving? Call 1-800-etc."

These companies ask for constant evaluation. Why? Because they know that feedback and correction from their customers will make them better companies. Foolish companies refuse to change or heed customer input until it's almost too late. (How long did it take Detroit to get the message that Americans simply wanted a *reliable* small car?)

What then, makes for a wiser family? Do you mail out evaluation forms to your relatives and neighbors? Maybe print an 800 number on the back of your mini-van? *What do you think of our parenting skills? Call 1-800-GET-NOSY.*

Probably not. But for countless families we've observed across America, wisdom is spelled A-C-C-O-U-N-T-A-B-I-L-I-T-Y.

Both Gary and I have the freedom to hold each other accountable—and to use that freedom in a loving way. Perhaps it's a conversation on the plane after a conference about an attitude that's out of sync, or a walk around our office for a heart-to-heart talk. We're committed to each other for life as friends, and that means we have permission to give praise and correction when needed.

How we wish that many of those who come to us for counseling had a friend, relative...anyone who would lovingly hold them accountable.

If the family in the opening story of this chapter had experienced the love, support, and accountability of several other families who knew and loved them enough to confront their narrow, misguided attitudes about illness and the value of life, three generations might have been spared years of shame and grief.

I (Gary) am reminded of another family, and how accountability is helping this family history read much differently from the story we've just related.

My friends Ray and Denise came within a millimeter of becoming yet one more weary divorce statistic. Ray was a railroad engineer who tried to muscle his family with the same heavy hand he used on his diesel locomotives. Hot-tempered, negative, and verbally abusive, he had gradually alienated his kids and was on the verge of derailing his marriage.

Denise had her own struggles. Dark emotions from a sexually abusive childhood kept pulling her back into withdrawal and depression. Both Ray and Denise became Christians, yet continued to wrestle with problems from their past that seemed to be pulling their family apart.

But something different happened in this family.

Ray and Denise faced up to the problems in their home. At the prompting of God's Spirit, they recognized the obstacles and sought out correction—first through individual counseling and then in the context of a small support group.

## ACCOUNTABILITY COMES WRAPPED IN SMALL GROUPS

Despite good counseling, it hasn't been easy for Ray. He still blasts through the front door like a freight train at times, sending everyone scattering for their lives. But within the confines of a loving, supportive small group, he admits his weaknesses and asks for input and prayer. "What do I need to do to improve?" he asks his new friends. "What can I do to change?"

Within this group of half a dozen Christian couples, Ray and Denise are finding a measure of commitment and loving correction they have never experienced in their married life. People in the group love each other, hug each other, and constantly pray for each other. And once a week, in front of these caring, concerned people, everyone in the group has to answer questions like: *How are you two doing this week? How's it going this week in your marriage? How's it going with the kids?*

Ray came into his group meeting recently and said he didn't want to talk. "I've had a ROTTEN week," he admitted to the group. "I've completely blown it. I've offended my wife, offended my kids, and I feel really down." Everyone in the circle poured out their love and support for Ray. Different ones spoke up and said, "Hey, this is going to happen! We're all going to fall on our faces now and then. We're still under construction. We won't give up on you and don't you give up on us!" Ray saw and felt the acceptance, and began to open up again.

Toward the end of each meeting, it is the group's practice to have every person say something positive and affirming about his or her spouse. Denise may have struggled a bit to think of something positive to say about her husband that week, but she did, and said the words looking into his eyes. Ray beamed, but then looked down and said, "Yeah, maybe I did one thing right, but it's nuthin' compared to how I've blown it this week. I have a long way to go."

But with God's help and the accountability of the group, Ray and Denise *are* changing. While I (Gary) was talking to Ray on the phone recently, he got choked up and told me about one of the most moving experiences of his life.

"Gary," he told me, "just last night I received the greatest gift I've ever received in my life. My wife gave me a new name."

"She did what?"

"She gave me a new name! A different name. It's going to be our little secret, private name that we use together—our affectionate name. She told me, 'The reason I'm giving you a new name is because you are so different. You're not the same person you used to be. And I want you to have this new name.'

"You know, Gary, a year ago if you'd told me this stuff was going to be happening between my wife and me I would have never believed it. I would have laughed my head off. But I was just plain foolish, Gary, and I just about lost my marriage—my family, too. I can see that now."

Ray and Denise sought out correction. It was difficult at first. And humbling. Yet what was that small discomfort and embarrassment compared to the years of love and companionship and memories they will share down through the years? *Only the wise seek correction.*

Would my friends have found the right path on their own, with no input or help from others? Would they have eventually blundered onto the road toward healing? Perhaps. But how many years might they have wasted stumbling down box canyons, dead-ends, and blind alleys? And how many of their children might they have lost in the meantime?

Scrutiny is a key aspect of a successful marriage or family. As Socrates said, "The unexamined life isn't worth living." But it has to be more than *self*-scrutiny. Scripture says that "the heart is deceitful above all things and beyond cure" (Jeremiah 17:9). We may *think* we're doing fine or making great progress when we've only been fooling ourselves. It is extremely difficult at times to make needed changes within the family. Let's face it, we all become myopic about our own shortcomings and habits and perceived strengths and weaknesses. Yet sometimes an outsider can bring a word of wisdom that would never emerge from within the family circle.

The best map in the world does you no good if you don't know where you are. You have to get your coordinates first, and then you can use a good map. *Only the wise stop and ask for directions.*

## ACCOUNTABILITY IS ALSO SPELLED "ENRICHMENT"

Cindy and I (John) have been in various small groups for over fifteen years. These pockets of encouragement and support have been a tremendous source of strength to us as parents and marriage partners. But in addition to these small group sessions, we made the decision when we were married to add at least one focused "enrichment" experience each year to our marriage as well.

Over the years, this has meant attending a number of extremely beneficial weekend conferences that I highly recommend. While there is never enough time to attend a seminar, Cindy and I have found tremendous help in spending even one night away from kids and the phone; focusing on each other and gaining skills and insights to be a better person and parent. Call it continuing education for successful couples and families, but I feel it's a crucial aspect of keeping the lights on in your home.

In addition, the past three years, Cindy and I also decided to pay for six "enrichment counseling" sessions with a close friend and exceptional counselor, Dr. Bill Retts. After years of counseling others and encouraging hundreds of people to go into counseling themselves, I thought it would be a good idea to sit on the other side of the counseling room for a change.

I'll admit to you, that the first time Cindy and I sat down with Dr. Retts, I told him, "Bill, we're paying you for six sessions, but I doubt if we have enough to talk about for six hours." However, as soon as Cindy pulled out *her* list of relevant discussion issues, we could have gone into extra innings! And we have! Now, each year we make these six "counseling enrichment" sessions a part of our preventative plan to keep our relationship strong and growing. And believe me, I realize now that I'll die long before we run out of issues to talk about.

We've seen three things, then, that can help your family improve: small groups, enrichment conferences, and personal counseling. Yet as helpful as these experiences are, there is another important element of gaining wisdom that needs to be kept in mind.

## SKILL FOR LIVING

One of the principal words for "wisdom" in Scripture refers to skill in technical work or craftsmanship or battle tactics. When the Bible speaks of wisdom, it's talking about "the skill of successful living." It means *being skillful at life*. If you go to a wise counselor for help and direction, what you're really asking for are skills. Perhaps, like a proficient craftsman, he or she has honed those skills over the years.

There is a sense in which you can build skill. Yet there are certain skills you may never develop on your own. Imagine, for instance, that you are a "self-taught" cabinet maker. Over the next twelve months, let's say you construct a thousand cabinets. Yet if you build them all with the same structural flaws, you haven't gained any skill as a cabinet maker—despite all your diligent labors. So it isn't just a matter of "working hard at it." It is rather a matter of discovering the skills to make it right!

You may "hang on" through twenty years of poor family life, but what have you gained? A miserable twenty years. True wisdom seeks out correction and the kind of skills you need to bring encouragement and healing and growth to your family.

The author of Hebrews constructs a pointed word picture when he writes: "Strengthen the hands that are weak and the knees that are feeble, and make straight paths for your feet, so that the limb which is lame may not be put out of joint, but rather be healed" (Hebrews 12:12-13, NASB).

In other words, get correction, get back on the right road, or your stumbling feet may be permanently injured!

We have a friend who at the age of thirty-eight found to his surprise that he had a slight congenital defect in his foot. He'd been "walking wrong" for years, rolling his foot in a particular way that put pressure on certain bones in his foot and caused strain on his knee. He could no longer jog, and even walking was becoming painful. A skillful (wise) podiatrist, however, recommended corrective surgery along with special shoe inserts that would force his foot to walk correctly. After a few months, the pain in his foot and knee disappeared completely. He's not only walking without pain, he's *running* again, and loving it!

Simply walking more on that foot would have *never* made it better. In fact, eventually it would have crippled him. But skillful surgery and corrective shoe inserts released him to those activities he so dearly loves. It's the same in a marriage or family. You can limp along for years, hoping the pain will go away and health will magically return. In fact, all of your limping and pretending may be crippling your most important relationships. It may be turning out the lights in your home, one by one.

Can we gain the necessary "corrective surgery" from reading and applying the message of the Bible to our lives? Yes, definitely. In the same book of Hebrews we read: "The word of God is living and active. Sharper than any double-edged sword, it penetrates even to dividing soul and spirit, joints and marrow; it judges the thoughts and attitudes of the heart" (4:12). Paul expressed similar sentiments to his young friend Timothy when he wrote: "All scripture is inspired by God and is useful for teaching the faith and correcting error, for resetting the direction of a man's life and training him in good living" (2 Timothy 3:16, Phillips).

So we can gain life skills by humbly opening God's Word and praying, "God, please correct me and teach me." Yet when it comes to putting those truths to work consistently, we've found that accountability to another person or small group infuses those skills into daily living like nothing else we know.

A successful film producer told us recently, "I've collected all kinds of information about handling money and what I'm supposed to do about personal finances. But I wasn't doing anything with it! I never took the time to really do financially what *I knew I needed to do* until I got into a small group of people who studied a simple financial plan together. It was nothing 'new' to me in terms of content, but week after week we put that plan into action. I actually began doing the things that I knew I should do. I was getting support and I was being held accountable."

## HOW DO YOU FIND ACCOUNTABILITY?

It begins with the first big step of letting someone close enough to you to know what you're really like. Everyone looks good on a Sunday morning at church. But we also need those small group settings where we can openly and honestly share the temptations and struggles we face.

Several years ago, Gary and I saw a disturbing pattern. Many men we knew in parachurch ministries were not only falling from the ministry, but hurting numerous people in the process. As we looked at these men's lives more closely, one consistent theme surfaced: They had all moved away from honest accountability. There was no one—not a board, not friends, not employees, not even their pastor—who was willing to look beyond the facade into the real pressures and struggles they faced.

With that realization came a determination to do something about it. Since that time, we've not only been in small accountability groups ourselves, but we've given several men across the country a "blank check" when it comes to correcting us and asking those "hard questions" that need to be asked.

It's not easy to have John Nieder call and ask where our spiritual lives have been the past month...or to have Rolf Zettersten point out an attitude that needs looking at...but each of these men, and several others, have permission not only to call, but to show up on our doorstep if they sense or observe us drifting from our commitment to Christ or our wives or families.

Each of these men knows he has our complete permission to get involved in our lives in this way. As King David said so well: "Let a righteous man strike me—it is a kindness; let him rebuke me—it is oil on my head. My head will not refuse it" (Psalm 141:5).

That's just one method of personal accountability. We've mentioned small groups. Many churches offer and encourage such groups as part of their weekly fellowship. If your church does not, take the initiative to start one with several Christian couples, families, or singles. Set an evening where you get together for a couple of hours—with the kids or without—for the expressed goal of encouragement and mutual accountability. It doesn't have to be a big production. Simply ask one another questions like, "What are you doing as a family to build love and support in your home?" or, "What are you learning from God's Word and the books you're reading?"

Just being together gives a sense of relief and confidence. Somehow, it helps to be reminded that *all* families go through periods of stress and strain. All families face times of crisis and struggle and confusion. A weekly gathering with a group of people who love you, support you, and hold you to your goals will give you the courage and energy to make it through the week. That loving, subtle pressure keeps couples and families moving in the right direction—and keeps them away from dangerous side roads and dead-ends.

The Smalley household has some dear friends in another city who regularly "check in" on our daughter Kari. For years, they have sent her encouraging letters and postcards. Whenever they're in town, they take her out to dinner to ask her how she's doing with her personal, occupational, and ministry goals. Mostly, they just listen and affirm. But the simple act of taking the time to care about Kari in this way has had a profound impact on her through her late teens and early twenties.

You might be able to think of friends or relatives who could build that sort of affirming relationship with one of your children. Better still, *you* might become that "honorary aunt or uncle" for a young person you know. Your impact on that life could be immeasurable. Talk about minimum efforts producing maximum results!

Support and accountability is authentic love; it is love that cares enough to confront. It's a reminder that we're all fellow strugglers, fellow travelers on this sometimes perplexing journey through parenting. It's an admission that to keep the lights burning in our homes, we need the help of God and God's people.

No, you really can't make it alone.

You don't have to.

# PREPARING FOR TRANSITIONS

I

t was planned as a Thanksgiving they would always remember.

It became a Thanksgiving they would long to forget.

According to the plan, the family of six would gather for the holiday meal at a resort a hundred miles north of their home in Phoenix. After dinner, they would pose for family pictures at a landmark red rock formation in the desert. Part of the uniqueness of the day was the way they were going to arrive at their destination. The mom, dad, and young daughter would drive; the three sons, ages nineteen, seventeen, and fifteen, would fly in a rented Cessna.

The family rendezvoused on schedule at the resort, and dove into a sumptuous feast at the clubhouse. Afterward, everyone clowned around snapping "Wild West" shots out in the sun-splashed Arizona desert.

It was fortunate the pictures turned out as well as they did. It would be their last family portrait. The mom, dad, and sister reveled in a beautiful twilight drive home. But the three boys never made it home at all. A Civil Air Patrol plane found the wreckage the next day, strewn haphazardly across the sand.

The next few torturous months produced yet another casualty. Unable to cope with the grief and stress, the father moved out and sued for divorce. She got the daughter; he got the house.

Consider for a moment the avalanche of changes faced by the woman in that family. In less than twelve months she went from a family of six to a family of two...from married life to single...from a five-bedroom home to a three-bedroom rental...from a full-time homemaker to a full-time breadwinner.

Cindy and I (John) sat shell-shocked as this woman spilled out her story in our home. I thought of Job's three friends who came to comfort him after a similar explosion of change. Scripture says the three men "sat on the ground with him for seven days and seven nights. No one said a word to him, because they saw how great his suffering was" (Job 2:13).

We did what you might have done in that same situation: we listened, wept with her, and did our best to offer the great healing love of Christ. Much later, after winning the right to be heard, we shared something else with her as well. We took the time to explain three crucial principles that will help anyone facing major transitions in life.

Before we share these three principles, we need to lay out several ground rules for change. Things such as counting on change, taking early (mental) retirement, addressing contingency plans, and planning times of communication. Each can provide an important pillar in a family that stays solid under the pressures of change.

## LIFE EQUALS CHANGE

The woman in this story had to face a cluster of wrenching, rapid-fire life transitions in just a few months. While most of us may never have to endure that much change compressed into so brief a time, the truth is that our lives are always in transition. We're all pilgrims and sojourners on this little planet. Life IS change. The sooner we accept and *plan on that fact* the more fulfillment and peace we will enjoy in our families.

When I (Gary) was growing up, our family moved twelve times in less than ten years. With my "otter" temperament, I never minded the turmoil and mayhem. I just got used to rooms full of boxes and making new friends every month or two. I loved it. Whenever I'd find myself with a tough teacher in school, I'd think in the back of my mind, *Aw, let her yell at me and get all excited. I'll be out of here in a couple months anyway.*

My family simply counted on change through those years. Many families do not. So when the inevitable shifts and turnabouts come along, they spark destructive anxiety, pressure, and interpersonal conflict. As counselors, we've seen families crumple like wet cardboard simply because they did not anticipate a major transition. Instead of gearing down for a hefty speed bump in the road ahead, some family wagons hit them at ninety miles an hour and rip the axles right off the frame. It doesn't have to be that way.

### HANGING UP THE CLEATS

In our ministry we've spent a great deal of time with professional athletes. One of our goals has been to reduce the unbelievable divorce rate among these gifted individuals—a marriage failure rate near the eightieth percentile.

Why all the marital trauma? Think for a moment of that talented linebacker who has had basically one consuming goal through high school and college: to make it in the big leagues. So he nails down a spot on a pro roster and it's like Dorothy landing in Oz and Alice parachuting into Wonderland; the very stuff of dreams.

His identity is clear: *He's one of the best football players in the world.* That's who he is; that's what he's all about. Then a few seasons into this fantasy vocation he takes a helmet on the side of the knee and goes down with a career-ending injury...and suddenly this passionate, tightly-focused individual is lost in space! He no longer knows who he is. He can't figure out why he should get out of bed in the morning. The resulting tensions and strains rip his marriage and family apart.

This happens again and again, but so often it could be prevented through some careful forethought and planning. Obviously, this jock is going to have to hang up his cleats at *some point* in the future. You don't play football into your fifties and there are only so many network "color commentator" jobs up for grabs in a given decade. If the couple had looked up and peered down the road a ways, they might have been ready for life-after-football.

It's the same with all of us non-celebrity types. Life's game plan includes a good number of changes you can anticipate and plan on: first baby, terrible two's, adolescence, dating, empty nest, mid-life, menopause, grandchildren, retirement, etc. But it will also be filled with sneaky speed-bumps, strange detours, frustrating dead-ends, sudden lane changes, and unscheduled exits.

If you plan on both the major "expected" changes as well as probable unexpected changes, you'll stand a better chance of reaching your destination...together.

## CONTINGENCY PLANS

Not too long ago, I (John) spent an evening with my wife, Cindy, talking about what she should do if I suddenly died. Perhaps it was the story of our friend losing her sons in a plane crash that reminded me of all the times I'm in the air. But regardless, I felt it was time we had a heart-to-heart talk about the future—if I wasn't in it.

Was it an easy conversation? No. But it was certainly an informative one. In fact, I found out that in a number of major areas, Cindy wasn't informed enough to know what to do should some tragedy strike.

I got so inspired by our conversation, I went to the safety-deposit box and pulled out papers. I wrote down phone numbers on a special list of whom to call—from Gary, to the mortician, to our pastor. I even got out our little video camera and made a "taped blessing" to detail these instructions—and got choked up saying "goodbye" in the process!

Do I think a bus will run over me or the plane will go down? I can't foresee such a thing at all. Yet if it happens, my family will not be blindsided by it. Amidst all the adjustments, they'll know we've talked and planned in advance about the thing most people avoid.

As tricky as sudden negative changes may be, a rapid transition to *success* can even be more difficult to handle. Thomas Carlyle wisely observed: "For every man who can stand prosperity, there are a hundred that will stand adversity."

For over ten years, I (Gary) prayed for some very specific things regarding our ministry. Two years ago, virtually everything I had prayed for came to reality. *Boom!* Within a period of what seemed like a few weeks I had check marks by all of those long-standing requests. The Lord opened up opportunities to reach and help families across America in a way that exceeded my boldest prayers. Answer! Answer! Answer!

I was so excited. I was so fulfilled. I was so grateful. And then suddenly I was so utterly empty.

Quite unexpectedly, I went into depression. I achieved all of my goals and nearly went under!

In the midst of a book deadline, I took time to find a quiet retreat spot and took a long, hard look at my expectations and my future. Despite my fervent prayers for ministry success over the years, I wasn't ready when the Lord suddenly gave me everything I'd asked for.

Surprise failures (and successes!) as well as major, predictable transitions won't be so disruptive and potentially hurtful if we've considered them in advance.

## CONSTRUCTION AHEAD

If you haven't figured it out by now, two things are required in preparing for transitions: alert parents and *lots* of family communication. It should be an ongoing topic of conversation between mothers and fathers. If you're a single parent, it's something to talk about with some older-and-wiser Christian moms and dads who've lived through many of those strange twists and turns in the parenting journey.

*What transitions are coming up in our lives or our children's lives in the next five years? In the next year? In the next six months? How can we prepare? What books do we need to read that will give us the insight and skills we will need to ease our family through these transitions? Have we prayed about them in advance, asking God for His strength and wisdom? How can we help our family achieve the maximum benefit and the minimum stress through each of these change points?*

If as a couple, if you can't set aside an evening a week to discuss these sorts of things, make sure you at least get an evening a month!

It's like driving on a road where you see a big orange sign that reads:

CONSTRUCTION AHEAD, NEXT 10 MILES

WATCH FOR FLAGGER

DRIVE WITH EXTREME CAUTION

The wise driver sits up a little straighter, opens his eyes a little wider, and backs off on the accelerator. He knows that at any moment he might have to brake, switch lanes, swerve around a barricade, or slow down for a rough stretch of road.

That's a good way for parents to think about the months and years ahead of them. They can expect the unexpected. They can count on some bumpy, nerve-jarring stretches of the journey. They can anticipate sudden changes in the smooth, straight freeway. *And none of these things should take them by surprise.*

At the Smalley household, Norma and I (Gary) tried to look down the road as much as several years as we attempted to help and encourage our three children. We recognized, for example, that there would be some particularly difficult transitions during the junior years: physical changes, emotional changes, a tremendous identity struggle, vastly increased peer pressure. We wanted to be ready for those speed bumps and treacherous curves in the road. Beyond those tender years, we knew there would be a great number of changes occurring between the ages of eighteen and twenty-two.

In the area of sports, for example, I encouraged my sons by pointing out a family pattern that would help them understand themselves a little better. For some reason, the Smalley male takes a major step in physical maturity at age nineteen. I knew that Greg and Michael would not be motivated in lifting weights or getting stronger and faster until they reached that milestone.

I couldn't get Greg to do much of anything in high school sports. But when he was nineteen years old I saw a tremendous change. That's when he began doing hundreds of pushups and situps, running ten miles a day, lifting weights, climbing ropes, and becoming a very good athlete.

A few years ago, my youngest son was only beginning to lift weights. But I could see that he was not as motivated as he could have been in his athletic endeavors. Sensing his frustration, I told him a hundred times, "Don't worry about it, Michael. When you're nineteen years old, all of a sudden it's going to click for you. And that's okay with me."

Again and again as my kids have approached various transitions, I've tried to prepare them for what was coming, praise and encourage them through the times of struggle, and give them hope that they would emerge better and stronger and wiser down the road. "It's okay," I tell them, "you're going to get through this and things are going to be so much better you won't believe it. Just wait and see!"

## THREE ABIDING PRINCIPLES

At the beginning of this chapter I (John) mentioned three principles that I sketched out for the grieving woman in my office. I believe these three thoughts will help anyone facing a major transition in life. I can describe them in just six words given me by Susan Miller, a godly woman in our church who has a nationwide ministry to people in transition:

*LET GO.*

*START FRESH.*

*REACH OUT.*

Let me apply these simple phrases to something as potentially upsetting as your youngest child heading out of the nest for college.

*1. Let go.*

Make this goodbye a significant one. And make it positive! Some of our friends have had little gatherings or parties to honor and encourage their college-bound students. It's a perfect opportunity to give a parental blessing and relive some warm memories. Haul out some of the old pictures, slides, or videos. Have a few laughs and shed a few tears. Help your child to celebrate the passing of one important phase of life and the beginning of a new, exciting phase.

At the same time, you'll also be helping yourselves as parents find some emotional closure. Yes, this stage of parenting has come to an end. There were undoubtedly things left undone that should have been done, and other things done that you wish could be undone. It will always be so. Yet life moves on! As one critical era of parenting ends, yet another critical era begins...a period of young adulthood where your young man or woman will need Mom and Dad's counsel and encouragement as much as ever, though perhaps in a different way.

*2. Start fresh.*

What changes will this "new era" mean in your life? What new priorities will replace the old priorities? How will you redirect some of the emotional energy you've invested in getting your kids through the roller coaster of adolescence?

In this second step, you look around at the changed scenery and think, *How am I going to adjust to this new setting?*

It's the same for a family that's made a major cross-country move. You plug into the new schools, you find a new church, you accept the help of new friends or neighbors, you subscribe to the local newspaper, you plant a few flowers, and you begin to set down your roots. Instead of living in the recently departed past, you force yourself to admit that this is a new period of life that needs to be lived to the full.

It's like that heart-touching scene a couple thousand years ago on the outskirts of Jerusalem. The disciples of the newly-resurrected Lord Jesus watched their dearly loved Master and Friend ascend into heaven before their very eyes. Up, up, He went until they were all shading their eyes and craning their necks. Suddenly He vanished into a cloud and disappeared from view. Would He come out through the top of the cloud? Would they see Him as a tiny dot becoming a tinier speck in the great blue vault of the sky? Where did He go?

Suddenly they were startled by strange voices right beside them. In unison, they dropped their gaze from the stratosphere to stare at two men dressed in eye-piercing white.

"Men of Galilee," they said, "why do you stand here looking into the sky? This same Jesus, who has been taken from you into heaven, will come back in the same way you have seen him go into heaven" (Acts 1:11).

*Come on you guys! Why are you standing around gawking into the clouds? Jesus has gone into heaven. That era's over. But get ready! A new era's on the way, and you're a part of it!* Just a few days later their new Counselor and Companion, the Holy Spirit, came upon them in power, just as Jesus said He would. It was time for a new beginning.

*3. Reach out.*

So your last child has gone out the door, or you've settled into a new neighborhood, or you've finally accepted the loss of a loved one through death. You've turned the corner and made a fresh start. What now?

I (John) can remember vividly when my mother came face to face with the need to move on...and reach out after a time of transition.

I was the last of us three boys to leave home. My older brother, Joe, had married his high school sweetheart, and they were living in a nearby suburb. My twin brother, Jeff, wanted to be a scientist since infancy and had long since selected an out-of-state college that would give him the best education in research.

That left me to go to junior college, work part-time, and change majors full-time. Finally, despite myself, I ended up with two years of credits at my JC and the need to go somewhere to finish college. That's when the Lord miraculously provided a scholarship to a four-year college to complete my degree.

I can remember my mother helping me load my Volkswagen and how supportive she'd been since I first mentioned the idea of going away to school. She packed me a huge lunch basket, hugged me heartily, and I drove off with her smiling and calling out encouragement in my rear-view mirror.

*What a supportive mom*, I thought. *I thought she'd fall apart when I left, but she did great!* And that's just what I would have continued to think all the way to school in Texas if I hadn't suddenly thought of something priceless I had failed to cram into the Volkswagen.

I had already been driving for twenty minutes, so by the time I turned around, nearly an hour had elapsed before I unexpectedly returned home. When I walked through the door, I saw something totally unexpected. There was my mother, sitting at the kitchen table, crying.

We both sat at that table and had the cry I'd been expecting all along. And finally, when we could laugh instead of sob, she told me something I'll never forget.

"John," she said, "for all these years, I've poured myself into you boys and loved it." I couldn't argue with her. As a single parent—or any parent for that matter—I can't think of anyone I'd put before her when it comes to loving and encouraging her sons.

"But starting today, John," she said, "I need to find someone...or something I can pour my life into from now on. I need another purpose!"

My wise mother knew that the best way to deal with the major transitions she faced was not to sit and sulk. Rather, she made a decision that day to ask God to open up a new world of ministry for her. And her life has been a blessing to us and many others as a result.

Are you faced with a time of transition?

Now is the time to reach out to others.

Now is the time to make yourself available rather than retreating.

Now is the time to seek rather than hide.

No matter whether you're in a new church, a new school, a new neighborhood, or adjusting to a changed household, there will always be those who need you. There will always be those who will benefit from your friendship, your interest, your concern, your experience (remember 2 Corinthians 1:3-4!), your expertise, or simply your smile.

Let's face it, this world is a cold, unfriendly place for a lot of people. If God has moved you into a new area or a new situation, let Him use you to bring warmth and light and laughter into your corner of that world. People will love you for it, and you'll love it, too.

You never counted on the road being as rough as it turned out to be? It happens. But maybe you also never counted on a Friend who loves you as much as Jesus. For He Himself has said, "I will never leave you, nor forsake you."

# VISION

O ne of our friends (who's always bragging about the Pacific Northwest) likes to talk about his "ideal" relaxation activity for an August afternoon.

First, he takes his rubber boat and rows out to the middle of an isolated mountain lake. Then he stretches out in the bottom of the boat, looks up into the blue depths of summer sky and lets his boat drift gently with the ripples and the breezes. Sometimes the easy rocking of the boat and the whisper of wind across acres of clear, deep water lull him to sleep.

When he wakes up, part of the fun is to see where he's ended up! Sometimes he drifts into a little cove. Sometimes he beaches himself on a gravelly shore, or nudges up against the bulk of a fallen forest giant, stretching out its limbs into the chilly water. Wherever he finds himself, it's usually no problem to grab the oars and row back to his starting point.

One time, however, a strong wind swept him rapidly to a distant shore. Returning meant rowing *into* that wind. Not so easy when each gust tries to hoist the rubber boat like a big yellow balloon and hurl it backward. Our friend's effortless twenty-minute drift demanded a difficult and exhausting two hour return.

Drifting as a family can be something like that.

As the months and years go by, it's as though everyone were in their own little boats, floating slowly in different directions. Then one day you look up from your easy slumber and you're shocked by a wide distance that's opened up between dad and mom, between father and daughter, between brother and sister. You suddenly realize that a little bit of drifting has allowed a great separation...and it may be extremely difficult to close that distance again. Like rowing against a strong, cold wind of indifference.

Where you "end up" as a drifting family may be somewhere you never intended to land. Somewhere that's less like a dream and more like a nightmare.

How critical it is for individuals and families to develop a vision for their future, for their *reason to be.* Scripture tells us "where there is no vision, the people perish" (Proverbs 29:18, KJV). It's the same thing with families. Without a vision, families tend to drift and frequently disintegrate.

## WE THE FAMILY...

Can you imagine where our nation might be without its Constitution? Actually, it's not that difficult to visualize. You need only look at the tragic struggles of many Third World nations across our troubled globe to get the idea.

You wake up in the morning and, lying in bed, you hear a strange squeaking, rumbling sound out your window. Pulling back the curtain, you see a column of tanks clanking down your street. Soldiers armed with automatic weapons stand at the intersection, stopping cars. Flipping on the morning news, you discover your favorite announcer has been replaced by a blaring military march. *What a nuisance,* you say to yourself. *Another revolution. I do hope they get it over with fast. It's probably going to wreck the morning commute. I wonder if I'll be able to make my lunch appointment?*

What would it be like to open your morning newspaper and read that Congress and the Supreme Court had been dissolved, and that the Joint Chiefs of Staff had driven the president into exile and assumed absolute power from New York to California? What would it be like to wonder from week to week whether you would be allowed to meet with other believers on Sunday, write a letter to the newspaper, or travel from one city to another?

Many people throughout the world must live daily with that kind of fear, uncertainty, and frustration. Yet for over two hundred years, Americans have enjoyed the heritage and benefits of a group of men who toiled, anguished, and prayed over a document that begins, "We the people of the United States, in order to form a more perfect union..."

Through the labors of our founding fathers, our nation has enjoyed a vision of who it is and what it holds dear. For two centuries our courts have wrestled with the implications of the laws and limits inscribed for us by these men who so clearly visualized the kind of nation they wanted to plant in the virgin soil of the great American continent.

Families need a constitution, too. Just as our national constitution provides us with a deep sense of order and security (even though we may rarely stop to think about it), a simple family constitution can unite a home around certain fundamental principles.

We had six basic rules in the Smalley home, but it really boiled down to two. As our children grew up, we must have said the same words 100,000 times: "The two most important things in life are to honor God and to honor people. There is nothing more important."

The essence of all the Scripture, Jesus said, is to love God and to love others (Luke 10:27). Every other commandment is a "subpoint" under these two. Honor is placing high value on God or people; love is showing high value with our actions. We first honor, then we demonstrate it through loving acts.

Early in our marriage Norma and I (Gary) asked ourselves, "Why concentrate on a million commandments when there are two that sum it all up?" We made those two bedrock rules prominent in our home, repeating them to the children almost from infancy. With God's help we tried to put them into practice in front of the children and with the children.

We would say again and again, "You are very valuable, and so are other people." We never let them get away with dishonoring another person. That was foundational to the Smalley constitution! If the children did dishonor someone in a significant way—whether inside or outside the family—they knew there would be swift discipline. That was the only time we ever lovingly spanked; when it was an obvious, major case of dishonoring parents or other people.

Later, six simple family limits grew out of our two foundational principles.

1. We honor Mom and Dad by obeying them.

2. We honor others and our possessions by putting things away after we have used them.

3. We honor our commitment to the family by performing all chores responsibly.

4. We honor friends and family by having good manners and exercising responsibility toward others.

5. We honor all of God's creation; people and things.

6. God is worthy to receive our highest honor and praise, and His Word is to be honored as well.

These six guidelines represent the final draft of a Smalley Family Constitution that each of us signed and dated. In a real sense, it was like the constitution of a country. We discovered that having a written, objective set of standards greatly contributed to our family's peace, harmony, and security. (As of this writing, no one has overthrown the government!) The children knew from the beginning that violating those limits involved sure and consistent consequences.

Cindy and I (John) started using this "family constitution" method when our oldest daughter was only two and a half. Obviously, our first constitution was simple and full of pictures. But today, with both our kids, we have found tremendous benefits from referring daily to the little chart on the refrigerator.

For one thing…by any chance are you tired of being the policemen in your home? When Kari was four, we felt it was time she began doing a few chores around the house to start building a sense of responsibility. What happened instead was the constant need to remind her to "make your bed," "brush your teeth," and "empty all the trash cans into the kitchen can."

The war of words stopped with an addition to our family contract. We sat down with Kari in a positive, unhurried time, and wrote out her responsibilities. Then together, we came up with an appropriate penalty if she didn't voluntarily do her chores. Miss one chore, miss "Sesame Street" in the morning. Miss two chores or lollygag in getting them done so she's late for preschool, and afternoon "Mathnet" stays off.

Then we all signed the little "family constitution" and hung it on the hallowed door of the refrigerator. It wouldn't be fair to say that Kari has never tested the limits. There have been days when her two hours of television are taken away. But it's remarkable how that single piece of paper has become the policeman in our home, not Mom or Dad having to constantly nag or pressure her to get her chores done.

The use of a family constitution is especially important when it comes to certain personalities. Lions do well with family constitutions because they help set the punishment, and it becomes *their* rule they're breaking (not nearly as much fun as breaking one of Mom's). Otters think boundaries apply to everyone but them; so a family constitution is one of the few things that can keep them toeing the line. And even Beaver children thrive with a contract, because it's really a type of list—and they *love* lists. (I haven't mentioned Golden Retrievers because they're so loyal, they like to obey you with or without a chart!)

Getting a parenting "plan" is essential if you want to have a loving home. But so, too, is the need to learn how to define and fulfill our unique mission in life—that captures the vision God has given us to accomplish.

## THE FIVE M'S

Vision involves planning for success. It asks questions like, "Where do *we* want to go as a family? What kind of family are *we* going to be? What would *we* like to accomplish in the days and years God gives us together?" If families don't have a standard by which to measure their lives, if they don't have clearly established elements of a successful, happy, mutually satisfying family life, they tend to flounder, *hoping* things work out—rather than *knowing* what it takes to make a healthy home environment.

A number of years ago I (Gary) had the privilege of going out for a special dinner with a lovely young woman named Kari Smalley. We have done this a number of times through the years, but on this night I sensed the time with my daughter could have extra significance.

Kari, then a college freshman, had something on her mind.

We'd hardly started our salads when she looked at me and said, "Dad, I need help with my five M's."

While that request might sound unusual to you, I knew exactly what she meant. And what we discussed that night in the course of a three-hour dinner helped Kari face the remaining years of college—and beyond—with a strong sense of confidence and direction. Despite all the usual ups, downs, mountains, and craters of young adulthood, Kari has not had to struggle with a sense of aimlessness or confusion.

She knows where she is going. And she knows why.

The evening Kari and I spent together was extremely rewarding for me as a father. Norma and I had talked to our kids for years about the five M's. And now here was my daughter, on the threshold of adulthood, asking for some help in fine tuning several of those M's.

She had settled the first M a long time before—while she was still a little girl. The first M is *MASTER*. "Who am I going to live for?"

The second M is *MISSION*. "What does God want me to do?"

The third M, *METHOD*, asks, "How will I fulfill my mission?"

The fourth M, *MAINTENANCE*, probes the question, "How will I evaluate and adjust my methods?"

The final M, *MATE*, asks, "Do we agree about our mission?"

Kari had no doubt on the question of MASTER. She knew she wanted to live her life for Jesus Christ. It was the next two M's she wanted to identify as she began this crucial phase of her life.

"Well, Kari," I said, "what do you want to accomplish with your life?"

We talked about it. For a long time. Dinner and dessert were long cleared away and water glasses had been refilled several times when she looked at me and said quietly, "I think I have it."

"Okay," I said.

"I guess what I'm really saying, Dad, is that I want to touch the lives of children. I want to communicate to kids that they're precious and valuable. I want to help them discover their God-given potential. I want them to know that it's worth it for them to reach for the very best in their lives—because with God's help they can accomplish whatever they set their hearts on. So many kids are so beaten down and don't think they can do anything or don't feel like they're worth anything. I *really* want to help them see that those things aren't true."

She had never before put it into words like that, yet her statement came out with such strength and conviction that it surprised both of us. It was obvious the desire and longing had been smoldering in her heart for a long time—on the verge of leaping into flame.

She paused for a moment, then her eyes widened. "Dad!" she said. "A *teacher* could really do that!" In a flash she realized that the METHOD of teaching could beautifully accomplish the MISSION that so filled her heart.

Now, several years later, that's exactly what she's doing. Every day she stands in front of her second grade class in an inner city public school and looks into the very eyes of her mission. Kari has vowed that not a single student will leave her class at the end of the day without being hugged or encouraged.

Kari knows her MASTER. She's confident of her MISSION. She's up to her ears in a highly potent METHOD. As time goes by, effective MAINTENANCE will prompt her to reevaluate those methods. Are they still effective? Are they still accomplishing her mission in a satisfactory way? Are there any other directions she could pursue that might make her even more successful?

The time also came when Kari faced the question of MATE. Before she married, she had to ask herself some hard questions. Would marriage help her to achieve her mission—even though it might change her method? Would her spouse share her vision in a significant way?

Today, as I write this, Kari has been married almost three years. Before she married Roger, he met with me and asked me to help him clarify *his* mission in life. Talk about warming a future father-in-law's heart! We had a delightful time together. (Of course, Norma and I are thrilled that Roger and Kari have now given us a grandchild as part of their mission!)

Through the years, Kari has observed her mom and dad wrestling with those very questions of mission and vision. Again and again, through the ups and downs, through the moves and changes, through the encouraging breakthroughs and the depressing dry spells...we've asked and reaffirmed the answers to those questions. It's given us focus as a family. It's kept us walking together in the same direction. And now, as our children leave the nest and begin their own homes, it will give them a place to start.

### FAMILY COMMANDOS

Years ago our young family grappled with the question of a family MISSION. "What is it, Lord, that You would like us to accomplish as a family? We know that our time together on this earth is limited. We know that You have a plan for us. We know that Your Word says the two most important things in all of life are to love and honor God, and to love and honor people. We want to honor people by serving them, but what do You want us to do *specifically?*"

The answer didn't come overnight.

I prayed about it personally for a long time. We prayed together as a family. We talked to other families we respected, read widely, and tried to come to grips with the principles of the Scripture. As the months went by, we came to the conviction that *the family* was the most important element in society. So we decided together that if family was the most important element, then we would dedicate our family to the task of enriching other families.

I asked my family, "Do you really want to do this? Even if it involves personal sacrifice?" And they said yes, they all wanted to do it. Norma wanted it; the kids wanted it. So from the beginning of our ministry, our kids have been part of the team. I've never felt alone in our mission— even though there have been some lonely nights in hotel rooms in distant cities. I've always felt that Norma and the kids have had as much interest in the work as I have.

The METHODS changed through the years, but the MISSION has remained the same. Early on, we sought to serve the family through pastoring in a local church. Later, we worked for a number of years in a large Christian organization dedicated to helping the family. Eventually joining with Dr. John Trent at Today's Family, I began teaching seminars, speaking at conferences, writing books, and creating tapes and videos.

At different crisis points in our family, we've had to come back to our mission, asking ourselves all over again, "What are we trying to accomplish together?" When one or more of us have begun to drift or go our own way, we've had to ask some tough questions in our family meetings. "Are we still facing the most important issue of our lives—helping hurting families? We're a team fighting against the destruction of the family worldwide. What can we do to hang together so that we can fight that Enemy?"

We are an army unit, a Green Beret team fighting the Enemy that destroys the family. And to this day, my kids feel a part of that struggle.

That was *our* mission. There are many others. Another family's goal may be to enrich other people's lives through physical healing, or by raising money, or by helping foreign missionaries, or through neighborhood evangelism. The key element is to find that area of service that everyone in the family can get excited about.

If you don't have a clearly-defined direction as a family, other people or the crush of life's circumstances will tend to set it for you. You will find yourself the slave of other people and circumstances rather than following your own clearly established, defined decisions.

Drifting without oars may be a pleasant activity for an August afternoon in the middle of a mountain lake. But life isn't a lake; it's a river that's rushing to an end. Smooth, placid stretches of that river will inevitably be shattered by tumbling white-water rapids or crashing waterfalls.

And a drifting boat manned by a sleeping parent doesn't stand a chance.

# WHEN A CHILD WALKS AWAY FROM THE LIGHT

**W**hy, Lord? *Why?*"

Ben cried out from a heart so heavy he thought it would actually break apart in his chest.

Sitting near the fire with his wife, Jean, holding her hand, he said aloud for the first time what he'd thought a thousand times.

"Jean, *I stayed home.* I deliberately didn't take that promotion because it meant I'd have to travel. I wanted to be there for Jennifer. We took her to church. I coached her teams. I've prayed for her every day of her life. Tell me, *why?*"

There was no easy answer Jean could give her grieving husband. There was no salve she could apply that hadn't already failed to nurse her own pain. No handkerchief she could hand him to dry his tears that wasn't already stained with her own.

Nine joyous months ago, they'd seen their only daughter graduate near the top of her class in high school. Three months later, they could both remember a sweltering, late August day. After getting an early start, the three of them had made the three-hour trip to Jennifer's new home—a dorm room at a well respected university.

Jennifer had picked that school because it wasn't "too far" from home, and because she already had several friends in an InterVarsity chapter on campus. With their only child leaving home for the first time, the drive down had been hard—and the drive back even harder. But both Ben and Jean felt reassured about the loving foundation they'd given their daughter. With the Christian friends she already knew on campus, Jennifer's prospects for a wonderful four years were like looking down a long road at a series of green lights.

In actuality, things went from "wonderful" to "nightmare" at warp speed.

Jennifer had decided to take a part-time job to provide some of her own spending money while at school. She ended up at a popular pizza place near campus—her first "real" job.

At first, her letters home were filled with news of school and her excitement of sharing Christ with those at work. But soon the letters became more general. Then they slowed down and finally stopped altogether. It became rare to even catch her on the phone. Then came the phone call from Jennifer's roommate. A call Ben and Jean just couldn't believe.

Jennifer had moved out of the dorm—and into an apartment with a young man who worked at the pizza place.

The pillar of her high school youth group...with a dad who'd been there for her...with a mom who couldn't love her any more deeply.

And now she acted like a cold, distant stranger. Her cool indifference to their pleas to come home plunged a knife deep into their hearts on a daily basis.

*What happens when you work hard to leave the light on in your home...and you child walks right into the darkness?*

Why is it that some parents do everything we've written about in this book—and more—and yet must still endure the anguish of a changed, wandering child? What if, like Jennifer, your child never has come back to the light? What if two, three, even *five years* have passed with no change of heart?

We've taken a number of chapters to share proven ideas and thoughts that can help parents keep the light of love on in their home. But we know that for some, despite all their efforts at skillful parenting and conscientious memory-making, their child has tried to smash that light in his hurry to leave.

One brief chapter can't deal with all the hurt a parent feels in dealing with a "prodigal." But in years of counseling with prodigals and their parents, we've identified several principles that have proven helpful again and again.

### WHEN YOUR CHILD WANDERS FROM THE LIGHT

Perhaps your child has strayed into darkness like Jennifer. Obvious sin. Blatant rebellion. Heartbreaking actions. If you have felt the anguish and emptiness of watching your child be swallowed up in darkness for a season...

*1. Realize that Jesus knows the pain of watching a loved one walk away.*

The New Testament book of Hebrews contains one of the most compassionate, helpful pictures of our Lord Jesus in all of Scripture. There we're told that "we do not have a high priest who is unable to sympathize with our weaknesses, but we have one who has been tempted in every way, just as we are—yet was without sin" (Hebrews 4:15).

One common characteristic we see in parents of prodigals is an overpowering sense of failure. The parents feel these pangs so deeply, even though many have done far more to encourage their children than was ever done for them by their parents. Others live with the genuine guilt of knowing they "could have done more" when their children were younger. They could have given more. Disciplined more. Sacrificed more. Been more attentive. These are parents haunted by the thought they've let down their spouse, child—or even God. The lack of rest that comes to our hearts from assumptions like these can rob us of sleep by night, and cast a dark shadow over any outside accomplishments by day.

Did you realize that Jesus must have suffered many of those feelings of loss as well? In the Upper Room, on the night before Jesus died, He showed His foreknowledge as God had Him pointing the finger at the very one who would betray Him.

Judas had been part of the "family" of disciples since the beginning. He had shared the same boat with Jesus and watched the storm stilled, and the waters turn to glass. He'd helped fill one of the twelve baskets full of left-overs from a supernatural feast. For three years, he'd shared sleeping quarters and life on the road. He'd eaten His bread. Drunk the celebratory wine. And now he stood ready to put poison in his Master's cup.

The more alone we feel in our pain, the more we need to lock our gaze onto the love of God. He knows our hurt. He sees our tears. He hears our sighs. In the tear-soaked soil of Gethsemane just a few hours later, He anguished over Judas and the pain that lay ahead. The Lord knew the heartache of doing everything right (literally), and yet having a child of His walk into darkness.

The first thing we need to remind ourselves when a child ignores the light is that we don't suffer alone. The same God who dealt with the failures of the nation of Israel time and again, does understand us and can offer us daily comfort. And He's provided us with a powerful extension of His love and comfort as well.

*2. Seek strong support in others who have shared a similar pain.*

It is my (John's) privilege to lead a Tuesday morning men's Bible study at my home church, Scottsdale Bible Church. It's actually a chapter of "CrossTrainers," an outstanding nation-wide small group ministry to men begun by Dr. Gary Rossberg in Des Moines, Iowa.[1]

In this unique "twenty-twenty-twenty" format (twenty minutes of praise and worship singing; twenty minutes of instruction; and twenty minutes of small group accountability), relationships man-to-man are begun and built. Even more, I've seen time and again how God can use the hurt of one man to help others.

I think of Brian. New to the church. First time at CrossTrainers. But carrying the familiar pain of a son walking far from the Lord.

He sat through the "praise music" time, not knowing all the songs but enjoying the melodies. He was encouraged by the teaching time. But then he froze inside. *Small groups for twenty minutes? These guys all have it together. They don't know what I'm going through. I've gotta get out of here.*

But before he knew it, he was circled up with four other men. Just as he feared, they all looked totally "together." He would have bet that none of them had a worry in the world.

And then the discussion began, and he learned just how far he was off the mark.

The question I asked them to discuss that morning was, "What is one area in your life where you need God's encouragement *today?*"

Brian was thankful he didn't have to start the discussion. And he was shocked by what happened next. The *first two men* who shared around the circle, both laid open their hearts. The greatest challenge and deepest need for encouragement from the first man came from a wandering child; the second from a wife who had walked away from the home and into darkness. And while the other two men in the circle shared less heart-wrenching concerns, Brian couldn't believe that others shared the identical hurt he'd kept dammed up inside.

When it came time for Brian to share, he pried open his pain for the first time, and discovered two newfound brothers in Christ who promised to pray for him that next week...and one who even met him for lunch.

It does no good to hide from our hurt. The book of Proverbs puts it this way, "He who separates himself from his friend quarrels against all sound wisdom."

If you've struggled to keep the lights on in your home, and had a child walk into darkness, don't retreat into the realm of the foolish. It's the wise who share their pain...and see their sorrows reduced and comfort doubled. It's those numbed by embarrassment or fear who forsake a friend, and forgo tremendous healing and encouragement.

*3. Maintain an open door to your child—but a closed door to subsidizing darkness.*

When a child walks away from the light, some parents become frantic to "win" that son or daughter back at any cost. Certainly, it's not easy to deal with a child's anger, nor their indifference to our calls for them to come back. But "turning out the light" isn't the answer. Ben and Ann did that, in an attempt to persuade their children to stay near home. Without realizing it, they did just the opposite of what the prodigal's father in Scripture did.

In the Lord's story, the prodigal son had demanded his share of the inheritance, and used it to set up a godless life-style. Yet while the dad in that story gave the young man what was rightfully and legally his, his subsidy of an immoral life-style ended the day his son left home. Yes, the light was always left on for his son to come back, but there were no "entitlement" programs to make "life on the road" apart from God easy for him.

Ben and Ann decided differently. Not wanting to be "cut off" from their children, they financed an apartment for them, knowing full well it was being used in a godless way. Further, without comment, they even allowed their son to bring his latest girlfriend home on weekend trips, and share a room together in their home.

Parents can't make choices for children. But they can and should set appropriate boundaries...particularly in regards to what they allow under their own roof. In their rush to stay "loving" toward their children, Ben and Ann actually turned off the light of God's Truth in their home.

If you are a prodigal parent, remember this illustration: If you take a white glove and run it through the mud, the mud doesn't become "glovey"; the glove becomes muddy. By lowering their standards and allowing the "mud" of immorality to take place under their roof, this mom and dad didn't win anything with their son. In fact, they lost what respect he had left for them. He had wandered from their principles— and perhaps someday might have returned. But now there was nothing to return to. There was no light to guide him home.

We need to leave the light on by letting our children know that we love them with all our hearts and always will. But we can also express in a non-condemning way that certain behaviors will not be tolerated under our roof. Nor will they be *subsidized* by our continuing financial support.

The best way to help a child come back to the light is to keep it shining brightly ourselves. Not to dim it down or turn it off. While we're looking to Christ for support, being open to the encouragement of friends, and standing firm in both our love and our moral standards, we need to look beyond our own hurt as well.

### 4. Talk through the hurt with the other children.

We've spoken about the need for parents of prodigals to share their hurt with the Lord and with supportive friends. Yet there are others close by who need us to honestly face our hurt as well—namely, *the other children* in our home.

When Jim, the oldest son, chose to move into the drug culture and away from his family, his younger brother Jamie was even more devastated than his parents. At age seven, he went back to being afraid of the dark, and even had an episode of bed-wetting while sleeping over at a friend's house. His school-work suffered, and so did his motivation to play ball with his friends—particularly now that his hero and batting instructor brother wasn't there to coach him.

Children can grieve as much or more than a parent when a prodigal walks into the dark. As parents, we need to model for our children how we're handling our hurt—and help them deal with their own.

For Jamie, help came through a wise father who shared with his son a "baseball" word picture at a time several years ago when the World Series was being played.

Going up to Jamie's room after dinner, he opened the door to his young son's hurt through this key communication method.[2]

"Jamie," he asked, "the Dodgers were your pick for the series—right?"

"Absolutely!" Jamie answered. "You know that."

"Who's going to be in the starting lineup for the Dodgers?"

An avid baseball fan and card collector, the little boy rattled off every position and starter's name on his beloved team.

"Who's your MVP choice for the team?" his dad asked, deliberately averting his eyes from the three posters of a certain All-Star pitcher on Jamie's wall.

"*Dad...*" Jamie said impatiently. "It's Orel Herschizer! You know that."

"Now, Jamie," his father said seriously, "let me ask you a question. It's World Series time, and Orel's set to pitch in a few days. But how would you feel if instead of walking out on the mound, he decided tonight to walk away from the team and not play anymore?"

"That would be *terrible*, Dad!" Jamie reacted with all the indignation of a die-hard fan. Then his eyes widened. "You didn't just hear that on ESPN did you?"

"No, Jamie," his father said softly. "No, Orel isn't going to leave the team. But let me ask you a question. *Was having your brother walk away from the family like having Orel Herschizer quit the Dodgers?*"

Even knowing the power of word pictures, his father was shocked at his son's response. The picture of losing someone important hit Jamie all at once, and his eyes filled with tears. Soon the long-suppressed sobs came, and both father and son sat on his bed and cried about a son and a brother who had walked away from the family.

In that home, a key to helping Jamie deal with the hurt of losing his brother came with helping him "picture" his feelings. That word picture also became a way of praying for his brother, as father and son would petition God at night for "Jimmy to come back and join the family—and get back on God's team."

While we may be struggling with our feelings as a parent, we don't suffer alone. All those left behind need to process the hurt, and move toward healing.

## OUT WITH THE BAD IN WITH THE GOOD

Out of nearly five summers as a lifeguard, there were only two times when I (John) had to rescue and revive swimmers. In both incidences, reviving the victim came down to an old premise—*out with the bad, in with the good.* Out with the water and carbon dioxide, in with the fresh, life-giving air.

When our children are pulled under by a major trial, we as parents need to practice "relational respiration" with our children as well.[3] By allowing a child to breathe out" hurtful and negative feelings, we can help him or her "breathe in" the good air of God's love and healing.

Unfortunately, "relational respiration" isn't practiced in every home. Recently there was a powerful movie about a pastor's family, titled, *A River Runs Through It.* Besides featuring spectacular footage of fly-fishing in the mountains of Montana, it portrayed a captivating story of two brothers who took very different roads. It also pictured a common choice for families dealing with a prodigal.

The story ends with the loss of one brother who had opted to "walk on the wild side." But instead of processing the hurt as a family, there was simply a "stoic" acceptance of a tragedy that would forever leave a hole in their hearts.

It was obvious that there was deep love for the lost son, yet even after the young man's death, there was an unwritten "gag" rule enforced by the father. Instead of honest talks or shared tears *(out with the bad, in with the good)* processing the pain was left up to each individual in silence. Healing was relegated to veiled references to what "could have been."

How important is it really to get that "bad air" of hurt, anger, and disappointment out of a child's life? How damaging can "suffering in silence" really be? Perhaps a centuries-old story can help us answer that question.

In Spartan legend, there was a young boy who caught a wild fox one morning during his "study time." Instead of giving attention to his lessons, he was busy playing with the fox when suddenly he saw his tutor walking toward him. Not wanting to be caught and reprimanded, he stuffed the animal under his tunic.

As the young boy stood there with a blank expression, answering lengthy questions from his tutor, the trapped fox was tearing away at his insides the whole time. It clawed and scratched in its panic to get away until, finally, the boy fell dead at the feet of his instructor—and became a model for all Spartan boys to come.

The Spartan credo was, "Hold on to your emotions. Keep them in check. *Even if it's killing you,* don't share your hurt."

For Jamie, in the story we told earlier, the anger and hurt he held inside had begun to attack his schoolwork, claw at desire to be with his friends, and rip away his feelings of personal value. Left to fester in a home that didn't practice "relational respiration," Jamie could have been in for some serious emotional and spiritual damage.

As Christians, the example we need to teach our sons and daughters is one of honest dealings with our hurt and disappointment. We need to show them that even those of great faith practiced "relational respiration." In the psalms, David cried out in desperate anguish and distress to the Lord. Yet after breathing out his hurt, he always affirmed his trust in God. Paul asked repeatedly for the Lord to take away the painful thorn in his flesh. Yet after breathing out his hurt, he accepted God's love and the power to live with his pain. Even the Lord Jesus shared His deep anguish at Gethsemane—and then followed it with words of trust.

It's not wrong to cry out in hurt to a loving God. His shoulders are broad enough to carry our hurt, and provide us hope and strength for the day. Nor is it wrong to let our children honestly share their hurt. By practicing "relational respiration," we can keep our children from allowing unresolved negative emotions to push them into the darkness.

*"But you haven't told me how to get my prodigal back home!"*

You're right...and wrong.

Trying to force a prodigal to come back home is often as successful as trying to push a long rope. Picture an eight-foot piece of rope, and your task is to *push* it twenty yards down a field to a finish line. What year do you think it will be when you cross the goal?

But wait. Change the rules for a moment. Now you can walk toward the goal-line yourself, *pulling* the rope behind you. If there were a "rope Olympics," you could win that way in record time!

The same principle holds true in dealing with prodigals. Many parents have worn themselves out trying to "push" a rebellious child into a change of behavior. But what does all of that emotionally exhausting effort yield?

We may find ourselves locked in an interminable power struggle that becomes as frustrating as pushing eight yards of floppy hemp.

As we've said before, we can't make choices for adult children. *But we can lead them.* As we continue to walk consistently toward the light of a godly life, we can show the way. Walking in the Light carries the most power to change a child. Godly actions carry far more weight than our words.

Don't give up hope, dear parent! Remember that for many prodigals, coming home represents *two* giant steps, rather than just one. As you continue to walk in the light of obedience to Christ and His Word, coming back home means they have to face you *and* the Lord who stands behind you. That can be a big challenge for any wanderer's stubborn pride.

But pride can be humbled. It happens every day.

Lives can be turned around. It happens every day.

We've seen it happen again and again and again. We've witnessed it in letters and conversations with moms and dads from every state and province, and in countries around the world. It's always too soon to give up.

Our prayer for you is fourfold. First, that you will turn to the God of light and hope to heal your hurt. Second, that you'll share your pain with supportive friends as well. Third, that you'll model an openness before your other children, and help them deal with their own hurt.

And finally, that you'll leave the light on for your prodigal...without dimming it through unhealthy compromise.

We can't guarantee what day it will be when your prodigal comes home. For some, their greatest prayer request of having a child return home may not be answered until after they're in heaven. But we can guarantee that the lights of home will never shine more brightly than on the day a prodigal walks up the sidewalk to the front door.

It may be on a Sunday morning in May. It may be late one October night. It may be in the snow and twilight of a December afternoon.

Whatever the day, it's Christmas in a parent's heart.

Notes

1. To contact CrossTrainers for information on beginning a small group ministry in your church, write, Tom Vander Well, West Towers, 1200 35th St., Suite 507, West Des Moines, Iowa 50266, or call (515)225-0034.

2. For more details on this concept, please see Gary Smalley and Dr. John Trent's book, *The Language of Love* (Colorado Springs: Focus on the Family Publishing, 1990).

3. For more information on this concept, see the video series by Dr. John Trent, "Helping Your Kids Get Along!" Word Books and Videos, 1993.

# Chapter Fifteen

# WHEN LIFE
# OVERFLOWS

He had just one thing on his dresser. It was an Academy Award. And he hated the sight of it.

I (John) received the mysterious call from an agent of "someone in the entertainment industry." Would Gary and I be willing to fly to New York and counsel an individual who was severely depressed?

We were given no name. A mutual acquaintance, the agent told me, had recommended us. I called that acquaintance, and yes, he was aware of the situation and recommended we try to help. He further warned us that this celebrity hadn't eaten for days and could be suicidal.

*Good grief!* I thought. *Aren't there any counselors in New York?* But after Gary and I prayed together and talked it over, we concluded that if this was a door God was opening for us, we'd better not hesitate going through it. We flew into Kennedy International the following evening.

The next morning, when the cab left us off at a posh apartment tower, Gary and I looked at each other. What in the world were two Arizona family counselors with scuffed shoes doing *here?* We shrugged our shoulders, presented our credentials to the security guard, and went straight up to the penthouse.

After a minute or two of gawking at the lavish furnishings and original works of art in the enormous apartment, we quickly reminded ourselves that this was simply one more deeply hurting human being who needed help. We both breathed silent prayers for God's wisdom and went to work.

The story almost sounded like the plot of an old B movie, yet it was true. Here was a divorced, middle-aged man who had won nearly every prestigious award in his field. Yet he was desperately unhappy. He had been abused and beaten down as a child but achieved sudden, unbelievable stardom while hardly more than a teenager. In the first glow of this fantasy lifestyle, he married another "celebrity," genuinely hoping he would find happiness with this stunningly beautiful young woman.

That was only the first of his "expectations" to be crushed. In less than two years the marriage was incinerated by the demands of two flaming egos and two super-heated careers. A string of affairs with forgettable, ever-available starlets in the years to come did nothing to erase the sense of failure or fill the aching emptiness. He concentrated instead on another goal.

He wanted an Oscar.

There were other trophies and honors that came his way, but this was THE award. The only one that mattered. If he could just win an Academy Award, that would be his crowning achievement. That would give his life meaning. That would usher in the sense of satisfaction that somehow seemed always just out of reach.

And then the very worst thing happened. He actually won an Oscar. It gleamed now in solitary glory on an otherwise naked dresser top. *And it did absolutely nothing for him.* There was nothing left to live for. Nothing more to attain. Nowhere else to go.

Did "religion" have anything for him? Did Jesus Christ? In his personal screening room, he watched a private copy of "The Greatest Story Ever Told." He watched it again and again and again. Was there something...Someone there? Someone who loved him for who he was and not for what he had accomplished?

170

## THREE WELLS

You may never know the letdown that can come after winning an Oscar, Emmy, or Grammy, but you may find yourself just as disappointed at some point in your life...just as empty...just as unfulfilled. I (Gary) recently counseled a homemaker in Dallas, Texas. She lives in a beautiful, sprawling ranch-style home in an exclusive suburb. She has everything she's always wanted since she was a little girl playing Barbies and watching *Cinderella*. Marriage. Kids. Home. Cars. Clothes. Friends. Wealth. And she feels totally hollow.

Children can experience the same phenomenon. Ultimately, that gleaming new bike will get scraped up or stolen. The new puppy will puddle up the kitchen floor. The new boyfriend or girlfriend will suddenly forget his or her assertions of undying love and seek fresh horizons.

Disappointed expectations confront all of us. *How you handle those disappointments as a parent will have a powerful impact on the peace and stability of your home.*

Over the last few years, we have been presenting people around the country with a simple word picture that describes how that deep inner thirst may be satisfied. One of my (Gary's) previous books, *Joy That Lasts*, explains that search for fulfillment in detail. But let's take just a moment over the next few pages to introduce a concept that may be the most important of all home remedies.

Most people want to drink from the goodness of life, thinking those "good things" will bring satisfaction. It's as though we take a rope, tie it to a bucket, and throw it into three different wells.

One well has a sign posted over the top that reads, "Others." We throw our bucket into that well, hoping and expecting to find our thirst fully satisfied. To our dismay, many of us find we are still thirsty. Or that the water is somehow bitter and undrinkable. Or that other people seem to be drilling holes in our bucket so that we lose the little water that was there. We walk away from this well disillusioned and unsatisfied.

Next we may throw our bucket into a well labeled "Locations." We try to drink from the well of a beautiful home or an exciting vacation.

LEAVING THE LIGHT ON

Maybe to us, it's as big as winning an Oscar. We try to get fulfillment from living in a certain place, and it just doesn't do it in the long run. It isn't as satisfying as we anticipated. We walk away feeling as empty and thirsty as ever.

A third well most of us try has a sign above it that says "Things." We think, *If I could just make more money, get a new car, or land a better job, I'd finally feel good about life.* Yet like the broken, despondent man we met in New York, neither material things nor awards nor status seem to satisfy that deep inner craving. We leave the third well and think, *Maybe I need to take my empty bucket back to that first well. Maybe what I need is a relationship, an affair, a new friend, a new person in my life.* And we start the unhappy search all over again.

The whole message of this little word picture is that the more we seek to dip into others, locations, and things to fill us with happiness or satisfaction, the more we're going to be disappointed.

At some point in each life's journey, we grind our fenders into something like a cement retaining wall. It's the hard, unyielding fact that "life is not fulfilling." To the contrary, it is often unjust, unpalatable, and rarely lives up to its billing. We can *never* siphon enough emotional energy or sense of significance from others, locations, or things to keep our personal buckets overflowing. Even though billboards promise "You'll be satisfied," we never are.

In fact, by so diligently pursuing people, places, and things, we end up with the very feelings of anxiety, fear, uncertainty, and confusion we've been trying to avoid. Nothing falls as hard or shatters into as many pieces as a high expectation that runs headlong into cold reality.

If your ultimate goal in a marriage or in a family is to say to your husband or wife or children, "I need life from you. Will you meet my needs and keep my bucket full?" you are asking for huge problems...and profound disappointment.

It's easy to find examples in every family of how we look to others, locations, and things for fulfillment. Parents often attempt to live vicariously through the successes of their children. Dad may be a frustrated athlete pushing his son to star in Little League. Mom may have dreamed of singing at the Met and so nags her daughter to practice music for hours every day. A parent wanting a child to land a lucrative career demands straight A's in school so that she'll qualify for a scholarship at one of the "right" schools.

A child may face the same dilemma. He desperately wants the approval of his father, so he's crushed when dad fails to praise his three hits in the game—but instead criticizes him for striking out the fourth time. We counsel scores of adults who are still desperately trying to achieve the approval of their parents. If they could only gain that approval, they reason, their bucket would finally be filled.

Lacking parental acceptance, children may look for happiness in things like computer games, fashionably correct clothing, a group of friends, or a complete stereo system for their room. They learn soon enough that they never have enough "stuff," so they beg for more. The pattern may haunt them into adulthood. Other kids may reason a *place* will fill their buckets—any place but home! So they run away, or apply to a college across the country, or take a job and find a run-down apartment with a friend.

Single parents may face the most acute problem. Many have already been deeply hurt in a relationship. Add to that the financial limitations that keep them from providing all they would desire for their kids and you have a recipe for bitterness and depression. Unless these parents find a consistent source of joy outside of their human circumstances, life can seem very bleak indeed.

Our celebrity friend in New York, for all the people in his life, for all the places he had seen, for all the material wealth he'd accumulated, experienced a raging thirst for something he couldn't even identify. Many of his high-flying friends had found that cocaine or alcohol, while not quenching that thirst, could dull its pangs.

Where, then, is the source of joy?

If others, locations, and things will never fill our buckets, where do we go? We spent a number of hours with the actor in his penthouse over the next two days. He talked and talked about his emptiness and his search. But every time we came close to touching upon the answer, there would be some interruption. A phone call from his agent. Another call from his investment broker. An interior decorator at the door. A California Real Estate agent on another line with the lowdown on a Malibu condo.

We knew what this man so desperately needed, but he never gave us the chance to lead him to the Well. The only Well that could ever satisfy his need.

"Everyone who drinks this water will be thirsty again, but whoever drinks the water I give him will never thirst. Indeed, the water I give him will become in him a spring of water welling up to eternal life" (John 4:13-14).

Jesus Christ is that Living Water. And when we dip into Christ and drink from Him, it becomes a well of water within us that continually overflows.

How then, can you bring this unfailing spring of refreshment into your home?

*1. Surrender your expectations.*

It's quite simple, really. When you're disappointed with life, *stop and ask what you are expecting to make you happy.* You can do this individually, or as a family. Is the family disappointed and impatient because the VCR has been out of order too long? Hey, if you're depending on that little hunk of plastic and metal to bring happiness, disappointment is inevitable! Is anyone complaining about how cramped the home is? A new, bigger home will only bring temporary happiness, at best. Is one of the kids hurt and upset because a "best friend" proved fickle? It hurts, but that's what happens when you hang all your expectations on another person.

We're not suggesting it's wrong to enjoy others, locations, or things. The problem comes when we require lasting happiness from them. Anytime you are angry, bitter, disappointed, or depressed, stop and see if you can identify your misplaced expectation. When you do, release it! It might even help to say out loud, "I value my friend, but I can't expect her to make me happy" or, "I like watching movies on the VCR, but it doesn't bring me lasting joy."

*2. Let God be the source of your joy.*

It's not enough to say we have wrong expectations. We must also embrace God's solution. The Lord put that matter clearly to the prophet Jeremiah many centuries ago: "My people have committed two evils: they have forsaken Me, the Fountain of living waters, and they have hewn out for themselves cisterns, broken cisterns, which cannot hold water" (Jeremiah 2:13, MLB).

We're thirsty for two reasons: first, because we have turned away from the Fountain of living waters; and second, because we have tried to dig our own wells…wells which continually run dry. The solution? Quit wearing yourself out! Come back to God, the unfailing Fountain, and let Him fill your life to overflowing.

Come, all you who are thirsty,
    come to the waters;
and you who have no money,
    come, buy and eat!…
Why spend money on what is not bread,
    and your labor on what does not satisfy?
Listen, listen to me, and eat what is good,
    and your soul will delight in the richest of fare.
Give ear and come to me;
    hear me, that your soul may live.
You will go out in joy
    and be led forth in peace
(Isaiah 55:1-3a,12a).

And just to make sure you don't forget the services the Great Physician is offering, we'll leave you with the slogan embossed on all His business cards. It's a slogan we think is worth remembering: "I have come that they may have life, and have it to the full" (John 10:10).

# Chapter Sixteen

# WATCHING
# FOR THE
# SUNLIGHT

Something unavoidable occurs in the life of every person or family…and it feels a lot like being stuck in day after day of dreary weather. Those who grow up in the Pacific Northwest get used to the idea of bidding the sun farewell from October through May. Of course, to be fair, that's not always the case. Sometimes it's from September through June.

Portland, Oregon, hosts a beautiful rose festival and parade during the first week of June. If you're into "raindrops on roses" it's the perfect event. More than once over the years it's been the only parade where the floats on the street actually do!

I (Gary) grew up in a small town in western Washington state. Every fall and winter I would walk to and from school under a heavy, ever-present blanket of gray. Sometimes the grayness seemed to seep into everything—trees, bushes, buildings, cars, cats, school teachers. There were days in December or January when I began to wonder if anything existed on the other side of those clouds.

Was the sun really still there—somewhere?

Was there still such a thing as sky the color of a robin's egg?

Sooner or later, however, the stormy Pacific weather systems rolling off the ocean would pause to catch their breath and I would look up and be startled by a tiny patch of brilliant blue. As the clouds would part a little more, a torrent of golden sunlight would suddenly spill through the overcast and splash across the road or playground.

Those momentary sun-showers would always lift my spirits. Hey, that big yellow ball really *was* up there! The sky actually *was* blue behind that dome of gray!

Even though I left cloud country years ago for the warmer climates of Texas and Arizona, I've never forgotten that sensation of bright sunlight suddenly puncturing clouds and washing away the shadows.

I experience it still, when I see God's faithfulness break through the gloom of difficult and hurtful life experiences. Whenever I find myself in the darkness of disappointment or puzzling circumstances, I start looking for the sun rays of God's presence and purpose. God has always been faithful in providing that light. The clouds break and—of course!—He's been there all along. His sovereign love and tender concern shine out like sun through a patch of blue.

Every family will experience its share of "cloudy day" hardship and pain. The Bible assures us of that. James writes: "Consider it pure joy, my brothers, *whenever* you face trials of many kinds" (James 1:2). It's not a matter of IF, it's a matter of WHEN. Dark days and difficult times are unavoidable. Although we may work overtime trying to shield our children from hurt, we'll never be able to shelter them totally from bruises caused by their own or others' actions.

As caring parents, one of the finest legacies we can pass along to our children is a determination to discover positive gain in troubled times. We can teach them to wait for the sunlight.

## STORM FRONT

Whether we like it or not, before they leave our homes, our sons or daughters may suffer through seasons of crushing disappointment or lingering loneliness. The sun may vanish behind a haze of doubt for days or even weeks at a time.

Childhood is filled with disappointments—probably because children have such high expectations! Adolescents often struggle with gloomy horizons. They may be let down by a friend, fail to make a team, get dumped by a girlfriend or boyfriend, struggle with self image, or fall short of their dreams and goals.

If a child doesn't know how to face the inevitable dark hours of life in a positive way, he may become emotionally or spiritually handicapped for months or even years of his life. However, the same Scriptures that assure us that trials are inevitable also promise great help and benefit through those trials.

There *is* sunlight on the other side of the darkness, and those who learn to wait and watch for it will not be disappointed. I (John) witnessed that just recently when I met one of my old high school friends at a conference.

What can I say about "Tim Terrific"? He was one of those guys who seemed to move in his own private pool of sunlight. He was popular, athletic, and voted "most likely to conquer the solar system." He sailed through college, married a stunning beauty queen, and went to work in a Christian organization—soon soaring to a top post of leadership. Then, following the arrival of two (perfect) daughters, a massive cloud suddenly left their home in shadow. Their third child, a boy, was born with spina bifida.

That was four years ago. Now my friend tells me that the birth of that little boy was the best thing that ever happened to him. I don't know how he and his wife worked through those long gray days of disappointment and strain, but after meeting Tim several weeks ago, I can tell you what he looks like in sunshine.

I could hardly believe I was with the same person. The old cockiness was gone. The shoot-from-the-hip conversation style had been left behind. He seemed more thoughtful, more interested in others, and more loving than I could have believed. Walking with his little boy along a steep, thorny pathway had filled Tim's heart with an unquenchable desire to help others. He left his high-level job to enroll in seminary, heading toward a degree in counseling. All he wants to do with the rest of his life is come alongside people in pain.

## SEEING THROUGH YOUR TRIALS

Does that mean we seek out hurt and hardship so that it can benefit our family? No need for that! We can be sure that life will bring plenty of low-barometer days. For that matter, there's nothing wrong with trying to avoid pain whenever we can. But it *is* wrong to deny problems, ignore them, or try to explain them away.

One of the all-time-great truths is that life is rugged and frequently unfair. The better we are at seeing through trials to what they can produce in our lives and our children's lives, the better we'll be able to provide calmness, assurance, and genuine love to our children...even when an unexpected storm swallows the sun.

In fact, trials are able to bring strength, maturity, courage, genuine love, righteousness, and perseverance to those who are willing to be trained by them (read Hebrews 12:7-11, James 1:2-5). The very things we fear might happen to our children can equip them with resilient strength, depending on their response to the challenges.

You have the privilege of explaining to your children that *every trial contains value.* Some have more value than others; some of the less painful trials may not be as valuable as the more painful ones. Trials are painful, but teaching your children to wait confidently for the light of God's purpose and plan can be a lifelong source of help and encouragement.

This doesn't mean shrugging your shoulders and muttering, "Que sera, sera, whatever will be will be." This isn't some kind of stoic fatalism or whistle-in-the-dark "positive thinking." This is the assurance of God's eternal, infallible Word...that He is present...that He knows every detail of our lives...that He deeply cares for us...and that "in *all things* [He] works for the good of those who love Him" (Romans 8:28).

I (Gary) remember a young woman I counseled in California not long ago. Because she had been sexually molested by both a neighbor and family member as a child, she had become extremely cold and aloof toward boys and men. Her awkward attitude scared away potential dates, leaving her lonely and confused. Although a Christian, she struggled constantly with guilt, anger, and low self-esteem. For her, every day of life was like waking up to perpetual dusk.

I spent hours with her over the course of several days, struggling with her through those traumatic memories and emotions. What value could there possibly be in those terrible experiences of her childhood? How could God possibly bring any "sunlight" out of such tragic and evil circumstances? Though I rarely cry in counseling sessions, I found myself moved to tears more than once. I could see such value in her life—and I firmly believed that God could use even those horrible past events in her life in a positive way.

The truth is, every time you go through a trial like the ones she went through, it gives you qualities of love you would otherwise never have. I spent hours explaining to her how valuable she was. I told her what a wonderful mother and wife she would be, because she was so incredibly sensitive and alert to pain in others.

The mother of an eleven-year-old girl had actually written her a letter, saying much the same thing. The mother thanked this young woman for the time she had taken to befriend and encourage her little daughter. "Because of your sensitivity and patience and love," the letter said, "my little girl will never be the same. I can literally see the difference in her life."

"You see?" I said, holding the letter in my hand, "you can spot a hurting person a mile away! You're constantly doing things for people. Just looking at you I can see the compassion in your eyes. That's why people come to you with their hurts. That's why these troubled little children love you so. They sense right away that you can understand and really *feel* their pain. In fact, your life reads like Hebrews 12:9-11. Because of the hardships you've faced, God has produced a harvest of righteousness (best expressed in love) inside your life."

Finally, she began to see how God could use her—was already using her—in spite of and even *because of* her terrible childhood. She began to smile as the tiniest crevice of blue opened in her cloud cover. It was enough. The sun doesn't need much of an opening.

## A CHANGE OF WEATHER

If you want to see this practice of "waiting for the sunlight" illustrated in the pages of Scripture, just let your Bible fall open to the very middle. When David poured out his heart to the Lord in the book of Psalms, he would frequently work his way through shadow and cloud and storm to the sunlight of trust, rest, and praise. In Psalm 13, he does it in the space of just six verses! Watch this dramatic shift in weather unfold below:

How long, O LORD? Will you forget me forever?
How long will you hide your face from me?
How long must I wrestle with my thoughts
and every day have sorrow in my heart?
How long will my enemy triumph over me?

Look on me and answer, O LORD my God.
Give light to my eyes, or I will sleep in death;
my enemy will say, "I have overcome him,"
and my foes will rejoice when I fall.

But I trust in your unfailing love;
my heart rejoices in your salvation.
I will sing to the LORD
for he has been good to me.

What a change! From groaning and mental turmoil and sorrow of heart to "rejoicing" and "singing"...all in one little psalm. Verse 5 is the key. David said, "*But I trust in your unfailing love.*"

In other words, "Well, Lord, the sky looks awfully black right now. Haven't seen the sun since I don't know when. My thoughts are a jumble.

My heart is so heavy it feels like it's going to fall out of my chest. Sometimes I feel like I could just roll over and die.

"But do you know what? I'm going to look beyond those clouds even though I can't see through them. I know You're there. I'm going to believe in Your unfailing love. And when the sun breaks through—and I know it will—I'm going to sing Your praise for all I'm worth."

### THREE WAYS TO HELP YOUR KIDS SEE THROUGH THE CLOUDS

How can you help your child wait for the sunlight in the shadow of difficult times? Here are three simple suggestions.

*1. Think carefully about your very first response to a difficult situation.*

Often, the first response by parents can set the tone for how traumatically an event will be taken. Have you ever seen a toddler do a swan dive off the couch—and then immediately look over at Mom or Dad? It's as if he were saying, "Hey, was that as bad as I think it was?" If the parent turns white, yells, "OH, NO!" and races across the room the little one will figure, "Yeah, I guess that was pretty bad. I must be hurt. I'm gonna scream." He's taken his cue and knows how big to play the scene.

It's the same as the years go by. Whenever there's an accident, a disappointing setback, a romantic heartbreak, or a problem in school, we've found that being as calm as possible and soft-spoken *from the very start* helps the situation a great deal. It gives them energy they need at the moment, energy to deal constructively with the problem.

When one of our children is hurting, compounding it by reacting with angry words doesn't help. If anything, such a reaction often pushes them deeper into anxiety—and also deeper into themselves—if they see that we "can't handle it."

Responding with initial calmness helps the child see that if Dad and Mom aren't despairing or flying off the handle, maybe it isn't such a disaster after all. If the child sees his parents unravel into fear or anger, he will be hard-pressed to respond in any other way.

The middle of an emergency is no time to draw up contingency plans. Parents who react emotionally with rage, hysteria, or cutting sarcasm to problems instead of having a plan for dealing with them will only make a bad situation worse. *Knowing ahead of time that God can use hard times to build character into our children's lives can help us keep a grip on our emotions.*

Calm, comforting words at the beginning of a storm prepare our children for even the darkest moments...and help them wait for the sunlight.

*2. Keep a watchful eye on your child's responses during and following the trial.*

What's the barometric reading in your child's room when the storm first hits? What does it look like a day or so later? After your children have experienced a trial, you should observe how they're handling it. If they're struggling, you can step in and help. If they seem to be "riding it out," you can drop a word of encouragement.

*"I've been watching the way you're responding to this thing. I know it's been tough, but I just want you to know I'm really proud of you."*

Be sure to take note of any early warning signs such as depression or anxiety that could mushroom into more serious problems later on.

*3. A few days after a trial, look for an opportunity to discuss how God could use it in your child's life.*

When is the best time to talk about "waiting for the sunlight"? How can you do it in a way that sounds authentic, not like you've been gargling with Nutrasweet? Perhaps several days—or even weeks—may pass before a child is ready to hear the message about God's unchanging purpose, plan, and love.

One way to bring up the subject is simply to say, "Are you satisfied with what you're experiencing out of the trial you've been through?" If he or she hasn't talked about it, almost always the answer will be, "No, I feel horrible. I don't understand why this had to happen to me."

At this point a parent may ask, "Would you like to spend some time this week thinking through this thing together?"

If the answer is yes, that's when you can discuss what God's Word has to say about hard times. If the answer is no, don't panic. Just come back another day and gently but persistently give the opportunity to scan the overcast skies and look for that tiny shaft of light.

A couple thousand years ago, a battered, beat-up missionary named Paul scratched out a letter of encouragement to a group of Christians in another part of the world. By this time, Paul probably looked like he'd played a full season as a running back in the NFL with no pads or helmet.

If they'd had ace bandages in those days, Paul would have resembled a spandex mummy (see 2 Corinthians 11:23-39). You like stormy weather? Paul was the type to sail his hang glider into a hurricane. Yet despite those constant hardships and hazards, he desperately wanted his friends to understand God's unchanging purpose and compassion. A few black clouds, a stiff wind, and a lightning strike or two didn't mean that God had abandoned them. Here's what he wrote:

> Thank God, the Father of our Lord Jesus Christ, that he is our Father and the source of all mercy and comfort. For he gives us comfort in our trials so that we in turn may be able to give the same sort of strong sympathy to others in their troubles that we receive from God. Indeed, experience shows that the more we share Christ's immeasurable suffering the more we are able to give of his encouragement. This means that if we experience trouble it is for your comfort and spiritual protection; for if we ourselves have been comforted we know how to encourage you to endure patiently the same sort of troubles that we have ourselves endured. We are quite confident that if you have to suffer troubles as we have done, then, like us, you will find the comfort and encouragement of God (2 Corinthians 1:3-7, Phillips).

Paul waited for the sunlight. He was never disappointed.

You won't be, either.

# Chapter Seventeen

# A FINAL THOUGHT: WHERE YOUR LIGHT SHINES BEST

**B**y now, you've received enough instructions on increasing family closeness to design a thousand-Watt home!

You've seen how to add brilliance by using affirming words, clarity by valuing differences, and sparkle by ridding your home of anger. You've seen how to bring the wiring of your home up to code by resolving conflict, and discovered how honor can illuminate your best efforts like a searchlight.

But before you put down this book, we want to leave you with a few thoughts to help you get "extra life" out of the love you'll show others. And to do that…let's take a look at one shining example in the pages of Scripture.

After six days Jesus took with him Peter, James and John the brother of James, and led them up a high mountain by themselves. There he was transfigured before them. His face shown like the sun, and his clothes became as white as the light.

While he was still speaking, a cloud enveloped them, and a voice from the cloud said, "This is my Son, whom I love; with him I am well pleased. Listen to him!" (Matthew 17:1-3,5).

Jesus was standing on a lonely mountain with a few of His closest friends when this "transfiguration" took place. But to help us understand how great a source of light and hope and inspiration it was for His disciples, let's look at this scene in modern terms.

Imagine a very mediocre college football team facing the unhappy prospect of playing the unbeaten national champions—on the champions' home turf. A thunderous roar greets the favored team as they enter the stadium. As the fearful visitors emerge from the tunnel and take the field, they see why their opponents are four-touchdown favorites. The champs are big, strong, fast, and almost swaggering in their confidence. The underdogs would give anything to win. But how intimidated they feel by the awesome team they face!

Then imagine...a "transfiguration."

As the out-manned visitors take the field, they suddenly see a vision before them...a vision more real than anything they've ever seen before. They see themselves...sweat-streaked and dirty, bruised and bandaged, but wildly *cheering*. In the vision, they're all looking at the scoreboard. And this is how it reads:

Time: 0:00

Quarter: 4

Visitors: 14

National Champs: 13

As quickly as they see the vision, it disappears. But while everything in the stadium still looks the same, they're different inside. Imagine the encouragement and wild elation seeing the end of the game would give them as they kicked off! What energy and confidence they would take into each quarter of play! They would happily absorb the hits, gang tackles, and bone-jarring collisions, knowing that all their efforts and sacrifice and pain would not be in vain. They were going to go home champions. They'd seen a picture of what could be...what *would* be!

That's exactly what the disciples saw when they stood with their Lord on that desolate mountain. All their effort...all their sacrifice...all the trials they would endure would not be hollow. Why? Because they'd seen the Light at the end of the tunnel. At the end of the long, dark passage, they'd caught a glimpse of how the game would end. *In victory. In glory. Forever.*

Those disciples got to stand in the brightest of all lights for a few moments, the light radiating from the glorified face of Christ, and it changed their lives forever. And as we reflect on this story, here's a final challenge to consider as we seek to keep the light on in our homes:

*The best place to shine your light the brightest is with a few.*

There's no doubt that these three earthly men were bathed in heavenly light. On the mountaintop, they saw how Jesus would appear in heaven. One of those men would live to make a direct comparison. In his later years, John was given a glimpse of the Lord as He appeared in heavenly splendor.

His head and hair were white like wool, as white as snow, and his eyes were like blazing fire. His feet were like bronze glowing in a furnace.... His face was like the sun shining in all its brilliance (Revelation 1:14-16).

These three men got a peek at the glory Christ will radiate one day when He comes back with His own, to claim His own. But why only three? And why these three?

The Lord could have chosen to be "transfigured" standing on the pinnacle of the temple, with thousands gathered below. He could have gathered all twelve of His disciples together as well. But He saved His brightest light for the inner circle; His spiritual family. For Peter...on whom He would build His church. For James...who would be the first to taste death for his Lord. And for John, who may have been closest of all.

In an age of rushing to gain favor, vying to increase our "circle of influence" and build an "image," this is a good picture to ponder for awhile.

Christ showed His brightest light to only three.

His closest three.

And He filled their minds with a picture of glory they'd never forget.

As we seek to leave the light on for those in our home, think about this question. *Where does your light shine brightest?* Are you an elder or officer at your church who rarely takes time to lead your own family in prayer? Do you give yourself to counseling, organizing, and encouraging the women in your Bible study, but find yourself resenting "interruptions" by your own children?

Just where are you at your best and brightest? Where do you *really* shine?

We've spoken with hundreds of bright, multi-gifted people over the years who have lit up major churches, week-end conferences, bookstores, communities, and air-waves. Yet all too many of these same people must live with a terrible regret. They may have beamed God's light into every home in America, yet their own families have fallen into darkness.

It doesn't have to be that way!

The more Christlikeness we can reflect *at home—with a few—*the more we'll bless the circle of influence that counts most…our families.

Those three disciples had seen the light; and they were ready to face the darkness of an evil world as a result. And that's the same gift we can give our children. In the gathering shadows of a godless world, we can help light their path, and make a way for them in whatever darkness they may face through the years to come.

That's our prayer for you as we close this book. That you'll radiate a warmth and light your family can't miss or mistake. May the love and laughter within your four walls beam like a welcoming light on a dark hill, filling your children's memories, drawing your neighbors to a life-changing knowledge of Christ.

Somehow, the light of heaven shines best through the windows of home.